ADULT READING IMPROVEMENT SERIES

READING POWER
BOOK 2

Revised Edition

BY ANGELICA W. CASS

MACMILLAN • USA

Macmillan General Reference
A Simon & Schuster Macmillan Company
1633 Broadway
New York, NY 10019-6785

An Arco Book

MACMILLAN is a registered trademark of Macmillan, Inc.
ARCO is a registered trademark of Prentice-Hall, Inc.

Published by arrangement with Monarch Press

ISBN 0-668-05969-9

Manufactured in the United States of America

20 19 18 17

TABLE OF CONTENTS

I Need To Lose Some Weight

1. I need to lose some weight.

2. I am twenty pounds too heavy.

3. My doctor told me what to do and gave me a special diet.

4. He said, "You must do special exercises and eat the food on this list."

5. I said, "I will do what you say, doctor, because I want to lose weight."

6. I did what the doctor told me, and I have lost ten pounds.

1

Use one of these words in these sentences:

lose

weight

pounds

heavy

doctor

exercises

diet

list

lost

1. I need to lose some_____.

2. I am twenty_____too heavy.

3. My doctor told me what to do and gave me a special_____.

4. He said, "You must do special_____every day and eat the food on this list."

5. I said, "I will do what you say, doctor, because I want to _____some weight."

6. I did what the doctor told me, and I have _____ ten pounds.

Write the missing words in the spaces below.

NOW	YESTERDAY
need	_____
lose	_____
am	_____
tell	_____
give	_____
say	_____
do	_____
eat	_____
want	_____
have	_____

Use all the words on page 3 in the sentences below:

NOW   YESTERDAY

1. I_____to lose some weight.   1. I_____to lose weight.

2. I must_____some weight.   2. I_____ten pounds.

3. I_____too heavy.   3. I_____twenty pounds
                                                 too heavy.

4. I_____my doctor I will do   4. The doctor_____me
    what he says.   what to do.

5. I_____the doctor my   5. The doctor_____me a
    address.   diet.

6. I_____I will exercise every   6. I_____I would exercise
    day.   every day.

7. I_____my exercises every   7. I_____my exercises.
    day.

8. I_____the food on my list.   8. I_____the right food.

9. I_____to lose some weight.   9. I_____to lose some
                                                 weight.

10. I_____a good doctor.   10. I_____a good doctor
                                                 last year.

4

Use these words in the sentences below:

ONE

pound
doctor
diet
day
food
list

MORE THAN ONE

pounds
doctors
diets
days
foods
lists

1. I lost one_____.

2. I have a very good_____.

3. My doctor gave me a good _____.

4. I exercise every_____.

5. I eat the right_____.

6. I have a_____of what to eat.

1. I need to lose twenty _____.

2. Many_____help people to lose weight.

3. Many people are on _____to lose weight.

4. I exercise seven_____a week.

5. There are many_____I can eat.

6. I have two_____of foods to eat.

Build new words:

ose	ave
h_____	g a v e
n_____	h_____
p_____	p_____
r_____	r_____
	s_____
ound	w_____
b o u n d	
f_____	
h_____	**eek**
m_____	l e e k
p_____	m_____
r_____	p_____
s_____	r_____
w_____	s_____
	w_____
eed	
d e e d	
f_____	
h_____	
n_____	
r_____	
s_____	
w_____	

Use these words in the sentences. Some words may be used more than once.

need

weight

lose

twenty

pounds

heavy

doctor

special

diet

exercises

list

because

ten

weeks

1. I have lost_____pounds in two weeks.

2. I want to lose_____pounds.

3. I exercise_____I want to lose weight.

4. My doctor says I am too_____.

5. I eat the foods on the_____he gave me.

6. I_____to lose some_____.

7. The_____gave me_____exercises.

8. I am twenty_____too heavy.

9. My_____helps me lose weight.

10. Exercise helps me lose_____.

7

Write these words in the spaces:

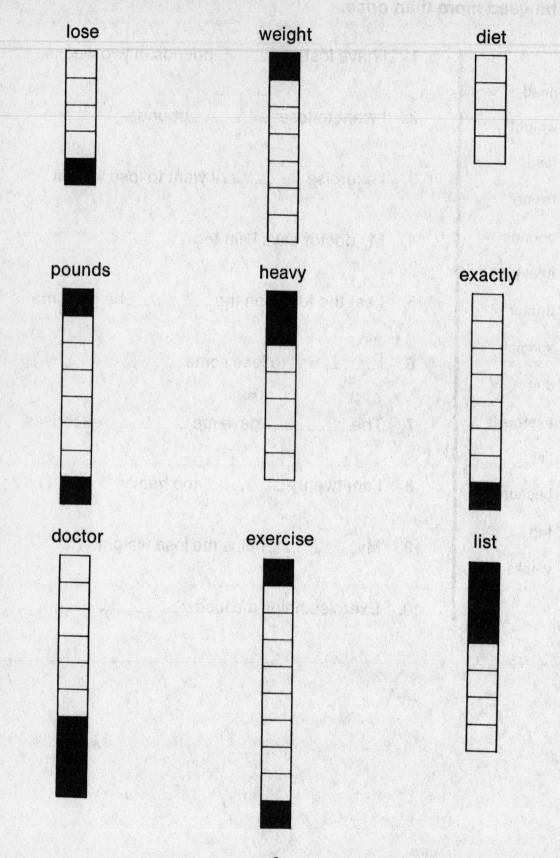

lose

weight

diet

pounds

heavy

exactly

doctor

exercise

list

My Birthday

1. Each month has a special flower and a special birth-stone.

2. There is a different flower for every month of the year.

3. Many people enjoy the flower for the month in which they were born.

4. Many people wear their birthstone in a ring or earrings.

5. People enjoy knowing about the special signs of their birth months.

Use one of these words in these sentences:

special

flower

month

year

birthstone

earrings

people

enjoy

signs

1. There is a_____flower for each month of the year.

2. There is a special birthstone or _____for each month.

3. Each month has a special flower and a special_____.

4. Many people wear their birthstone in a ring or in _____.

5. Many people_____the special flower for the month in which they were born.

6. Flowers and birthstones are the special _____ for each month.

Use these words in the sentences below:

YESTERDAY
was
had
wore
enjoyed

NOW
is
has
wear
enjoy

1. My birthday_____last month.

2. I_____a good birthday.

3. I_____my new earrings.

4. We_____the good weather.

1. My birthday_____today.

2. She_____a birthday today.

3. I_____my birthstone in a ring.

4. We do not_____cloudy weather.

Write the missing words in the spaces.

ONE	MORE THAN ONE
month	_____
birthstone	_____
flower	_____
ring	_____
earring	_____
sign	_____
year	_____

Use the words in the sentences below.

1. My birthday is this_____.

2. The ruby is my_____.

3. The larkspur is my_____.

4. I wear my birthstone in a _____.

5. Today I lost an_____.

6. Everyone has a special birth _____.

7. I am one_____older.

1. There are twelve_____in a year.

2. There are_____for all the months.

3. I bought _____for my birthday.

4. Many persons wear three _____ on one finger.

5. Last week, I lost a pair of _____.

6. There are birth_____for every month.

7. Next year, I will be two _____older.

BIRTHSTONES

January .... Garnet

February .... Amethyst

March .... Bloodstone

April .... Diamond

May .... Emerald

June .... Pearl

July .... Ruby

August .... Sardonyx

September .... Sapphire

October .... Opal

November .... Topaz

December .... Turquoise

My birthstone is_____.

Birth Dates And Zodiac Signs

January 20–February 18 .... Aquarius

February 19–March 20 .... Pisces

March 21–April 20 .... Aries

April 21–May 20 .... Taurus

May 21–June 20 .... Gemini

June 21–July 20 .... Cancer

July 21–August 21 .... Leo

August 22–September 22 .... Virgo

September 23–October 22 .... Libra

October 23–November 22 .... Scorpio

November 23–December 20 .... Sagittarius

December 21–January 19 .... Capricorn

My zodiac sign is_____.

Flowers of the Months

January .... Carnation

February .... Violet

March .... Jonquil

April .... Sweet Pea

May .... Lily-of-the-Valley

June .... Rose

July .... Larkspur

August .... Gladiolus

September .... Aster

October .... Cosmos

November .... Chrysanthemum

December .... Holly

My birth month flower is the_____.

Fill in the missing words.
Use these words in the sentences below.

NOW
is
enjoy
wear
know

1. Today_____my birthday.
2. I always _____my birth-day.
3. I_____the ring with my birthstone.
4. I like to _____my birth signs.

YESTERDAY

_____
_____
_____
_____

1. My birthday _____last week.
2. I_____my birthday.
3. I_____the earrings with my birthstones.
4. I_____the signs for my birthday last year.

NOW
enjoy
know
wear
is

1. I_____birthdays.
2. I_____my birthstone is the opal.
3. Today I_____my ring.
4. Today_____my birthday.

TOMORROW

_____
_____
_____
_____

1. I always _____my birth-days.
2. Now I_____my flower.
3. Tomorrow I_____my ring.
4. Next year I _____thirty years old.

1. I was born in the month of_____.
2. The name of my flower is_____.
3. My birthstone is_____.
4. My zodiac sign is_____.

Write these words in the spaces:

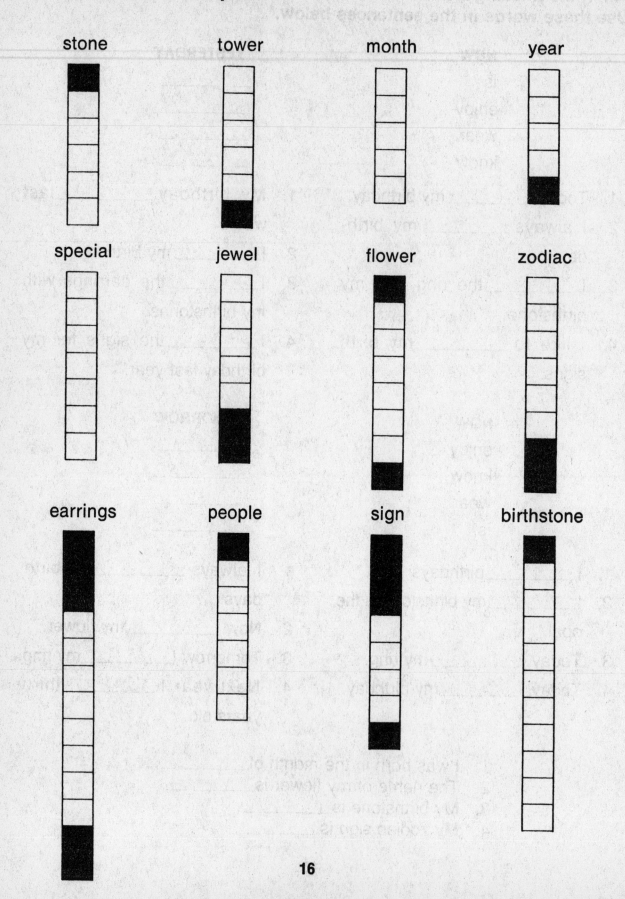

stone

tower

month

year

special

jewel

flower

zodiac

earrings

people

sign

birthstone

16

Hugh Wilson
1234 Fifth Ave.
Bayshore N.J. 20197

Mr. George Sanchez
987 Sixtyfifth St.
New York, N.Y. 10022

Samuel Adams   Patriot
U.S. Postage

I Mailed A Postcard

1. I mailed a postcard to get a free sample of soap.

2. I saw the free offer in my newspaper.

3. I wrote my address on one side of the postcard.

4. I asked for a free sample of the soap advertised.

5. Then I signed my name.

6. On the other side of the postcard, I wrote the name and address of the soap company.

17

Use one of these words in these sentences:

mailed
postcard
free
sample
soap
offer
advertised
address
signed
name
company

1. I_____a postcard to get a free sample of soap.

2. I saw the_____offer in my newspaper.

3. I wrote my_____on one side of the _____.

4. I asked for a free_____of the soap advertised in my newspaper.

5. Then I_____my name.

6. On the other side of the_____I wrote the name and_____of the soap company.

Read the postcard on page 19. Sign your name in the right place on the top card. On the other side of the sample postcard (the bottom card), write your return address in the upper lefthand corner.

Gentlemen:

Please send me a free sample of your soap.
I saw your ad in my newspaper. Thank you.

The Other Side

Stamp

This Side of Card is for Address

Pure Soap Co.

P.O. Box 1555

Chicago, Illinois, 16666

Write the missing words in the spaces below:

NOW	YESTERDAY
mail	_____
get	_____
see	_____
write	_____
ask	_____
advertise	_____
sign	_____

Use all the above words in the sentences below:

1. I_____my postcard.

2. I_____tired quickly.

3. I_____you have a new ring.

4. I_____my name on the postcard.

5. I_____for a free sample.

6. Soap companies_____in my newspaper.

7. I _____my name to the postcard.

1. I_____my postcard yesterday.

2. I_____tired at 4 o'clock.

3. I_____you yesterday.

4. I_____my name and address.

5. I_____for a postcard.

6. The soap company _____in my newspaper.

7. I _____my name to the postcard.

20

Use these words in the sentences below:

MORE THAN ONE	ONE
postcards	_____
samples	_____
offers	_____
newspapers	_____
companies	_____
sides	_____

1. I bought five_____.

2. I like to get free_____.

3. I saw several free_____.

4. I read two_____.

5. I wrote to five_____.

6. I wrote addresses on both _____ of the postcard.

1. I mailed a_____.

2. I got a free_____.

3. I saw a free_____ of soap.

4. My boy reads one_____.

5. I wrote to one soap_____.

6. I signed my name on one _____ of the postcard.

Use one of these words in these sentences:

mailed

postcard

free

sample

soap

offer

advertised

address

signed

name

company

newspaper

1. The soap company_____in my newspaper.

2. I have a new_____.

3. I wrote for a_____sample of soap.

4. I_____a postcard.

5. I wrote the name and address of the_____ company.

6. I_____my name on the_____.

7. I wrote the_____and_____of the soap company.

8. I asked for a free_____of soap.

9. I saw the free_____in my newspaper.

10. I saw the_____offer in my_____.

22

Build new words:

ard	ide
c a r d	h i d e
h_____	r_____
l_____	s_____
w_____	w_____

ail	ame
b a i l	c a m e
f_____	d_____
h_____	f_____
j_____	g_____
m_____	l_____
n_____	n_____
p_____	s_____
r_____	t_____
s_____	
t_____	
w_____	

Write these words in the spaces:

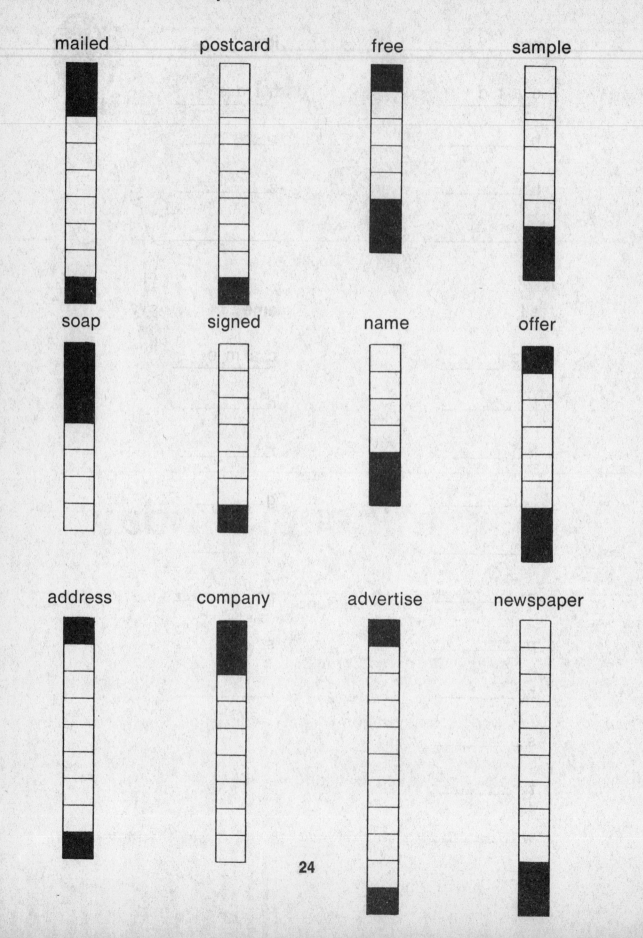

mailed

postcard

free

sample

soap

signed

name

offer

address

company

advertise

newspaper

How I Spend Sunday

1. I do not go to work on Sunday.

2. This is a day of rest for me.

3. I spend the day with my family and friends.

4. Sometimes we go for a long walk.

5. Sometimes our friends invite us to eat dinner with them.

25

Use one of these words in these sentences:

Sunday
rest
spend
family
friends
sometimes
walk
invite

1. I do not go to work on_____.

2. This is a day of_____for me.

3. I_____the day with my family and friends.

4. _____we go for a long walk.

5. Sometimes our friends_____us to eat dinner with them.

Use these words in the sentences below:

YESTERDAY
worked
was
spent
went
invited
ate

NOW
work
is
spend
go
invite
eat

1. I_____yesterday.

2. I_____at work yesterday.

3. We_____the day with friends.

4. We_____for a long walk.

5. We were_____to eat dinner with friends.

6. We_____a good dinner.

1. I do not_____on Sunday.

2. This_____my day of rest.

3. I like to_____the day with friends.

4. On Sundays my friends and I _____for a walk.

5. I want to_____my relatives to my home.

6. I like to_____with my friends.

26

Use these words in the sentences below:

ONE	**MORE THAN ONE**
Sunday	Sundays
day	days
family	families
friend	friends
walk	walks
dinner	dinners

1. I do not work on_____.

2. Sunday is a_____of rest for me.

3. My_____likes to take a walk on Sunday.

4. My _____does not work on Sunday.

5. I like to take a_____on Sunday.

6. I eat_____with my friends.

1. _____are my rest days.

2. I have several_____off.

3. Many_____take a walk on Sundays.

4. My_____invite me to dinner.

5. My friends like to take _____with me.

6. I eat many_____with my friends.

Use one of these words in these sentences:

Sunday

work

rest

spend

family

friends

sometimes

long

walk

invite

dinner

day

1. I do not work on_____.

2. I spend_____at home.

3. I go for a long_____.

4. _____I invite friends to dinner.

5. I like to go for a_____walk.

6. My friends_____me to eat dinner with them.

7. I spend Sunday with_____.

8. Sunday is my day off from_____.

9. _____is my_____of rest.

10. I go for a long_____with my_____.

Write these words in the spaces:

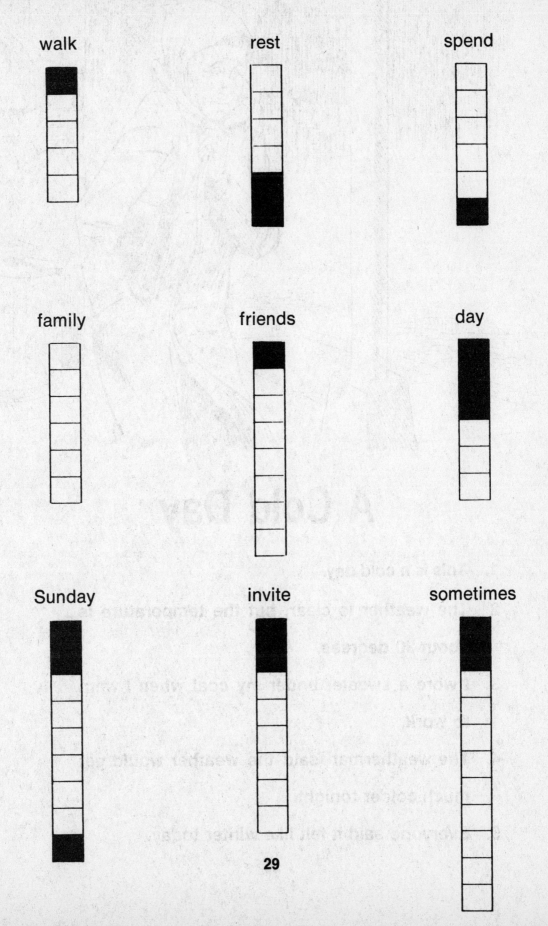

walk

rest

spend

family

friends

day

Sunday

invite

sometimes

A Cold Day

1. This is a cold day.

2. The weather is clear, but the temperature is about 30 degrees.

3. I wore a sweater under my coat when I went to work.

4. The weatherman said the weather would get much colder tonight.

5. Everyone said it felt like winter today.

Use one of these words in these sentences:

clear

temperature

degrees

sweater

tonight

winter

weatherman

under

sky

1. The _____ is clear today.

2. The_____is clear, but the_____is about 30_____.

3. I wore a_____under my coat when I went to work.

4. The_____said it would get much colder_____.

5. Everyone said it felt like_____.

31

Use these words in the sentences below:

TOMORROW	NOW
will be	_____
will wear	_____
will go	_____
will say	_____
will get	_____
will feel	_____

1. It _____ cold tonight.

2. My boy _____ his sweater.

3. I _____ back to work next week.

4. He _____ good-bye to his friends.

5. The weather _____ cold today.

6. I _____ cold by this evening without a coat.

1. It _____ cold today.

2. I _____ a sweater under my coat.

3. I _____ to work at 8 o'clock.

4. I _____ good-bye to my friends.

5. The weather _____ colder every hour.

6. I do not _____ cold easily.

Fill in the missing words. Then use the words in the sentences below.

ONE	MORE THAN ONE
day	_____
degree	_____
sweater	_____
coat	_____
man	_____

1. This is a cold_____.

2. The temperature went down only one_____.

3. I wore a_____under my coat.

4. I bought a new_____.

5. One_____told me the weather was supposed to get cold.

1. I like cold_____.

2. The temperature went down to 30_____.

3. I have four_____.

4. I now have two_____.

5. The_____wore sweaters under their coats.

Use one of these words in these sentences:

clear

temperature

degrees

sweater

winter

cold

weatherman

feels

1. This is a_____day.

2. It will be_____tonight.

3. The_____dropped 30_____.

4. It_____like winter tonight.

5. The days are cold in_____.

6. The days are not_____in summer.

7. I wore a_____under my coat.

8. The_____said it would be cold.

33

Fill in the missing words.

ONE	MORE THAN ONE
birthstone	_____
earring	_____
degree	_____
soap	_____
postcard	_____
flower	_____
sign	_____
Sunday	_____
address	_____
company	_____
temperature	_____
friend	_____

34

Check the words you know:

- ___lose
- ___weight
- ___pounds
- ___heavy
- ___doctor
- ___exercise
- ___diet
- ___list
- ___special
- ___flower
- ___month
- ___year
- ___stone
- ___birthstone
- ___earrings
- ___people
- ___enjoy
- ___sign
- ___zodiac
- ___mailed
- ___postcard
- ___free
- ___sample
- ___soap

- ___offer
- ___advertised
- ___address
- ___name
- ___company
- ___Sunday
- ___rest
- ___spend
- ___family
- ___friends
- ___sometimes
- ___walk
- ___invite
- ___clear
- ___temperature
- ___degrees
- ___sweater
- ___tonight
- ___winter
- ___cold
- ___weather
- ___under
- ___everyone
- ___feels

These are the words you have learned in alphabetical order.
Check the words you know.

a
__address
__advertised

b
__birthstone

c
__clear
__cold
__company

d
__degrees
__diet
__doctor

e
__earrings
__enjoy
__everyone

f
__family
__feels
__flower
__free

__friends

h
__heavy

i
__invite

j
__jewel

l
__list
__lose

m
__mailed
__month

n
__name

o
__offer

p
__people
__postcard
__pounds

r
__rest

s
__sample
__sign
__soap
__sometimes
__special
__spend
__stone
__sweater

t
__temperature
__tonight

u
__under

w
__walk
__weather
__winter

z
__zodiac

36

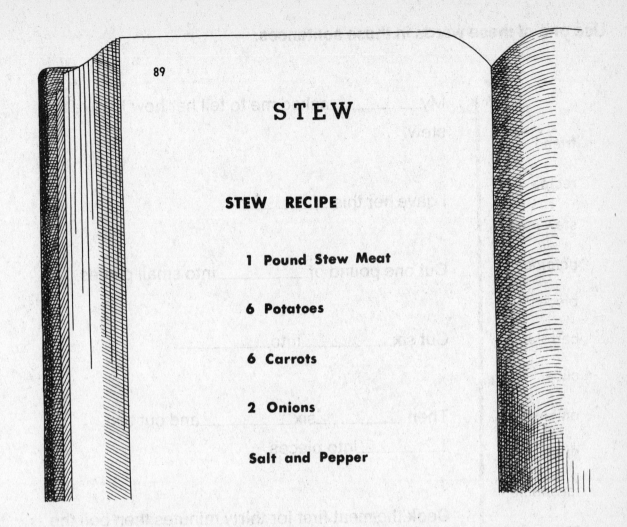

STEW

STEW RECIPE

1 Pound Stew Meat

6 Potatoes

6 Carrots

2 Onions

Salt and Pepper

I Gave My Recipe To My Friend

My friend asked me to tell her how I make my stew.

I gave her this recipe:

Cut one pound of stew meat into small pieces.

Cut six potatoes into pieces.

Then slice six carrots and cut two onions into pieces.

Cook the meat first for thirty minutes then boil the vegetables together for ten minutes.

Drain the vegetables then add ½ teaspoon of salt and ¼ teaspoon of pepper and put into the pot with the meat.

Cover and cook slowly for thirty minutes longer.

Use one of these words in these sentences:

friend

recipe

stew meat

potatoes

pieces

carrots

slice

onions

drain

teaspoon

salt

pepper

cover

slowly

vegetables

My_____asked me to tell her how I make my stew.

I gave her this_____.

Cut one pound of_____into small pieces.

Cut six_____into_____.

Then_____six_____and cut two _____into pieces.

Cook the meat first for thirty minutes then boil the _____together for ten minutes.

_____the vegetables then add ½_____of salt and ¼ teaspoon of_____and put into the pot with the meat.

_____and cook slowly for thirty minutes longer.

Write the missing words in the spaces below:

NOW	YESTERDAY
like	_____
say	_____
tell	_____
make	_____
cut	_____
boil	_____
drain	_____
add	_____
cover	_____

Use all the above words in the sentences below:

1. I_____to cook.

2. I_____what I think.

3. _____me how to make a stew.

4. I_____the meat into pieces.

5. Then I_____the vegetables.

6. I_____the water from the vegetables.

7. I_____salt and pepper.

8. I_____the pot.

1. I never_____to cook.

2. I_____I would make a stew.

3. I_____my friend how I make a stew.

4. I_____the meat yesterday.

5. I_____the vegetables.

6. I_____the water off.

7. I_____salt and pepper.

8. I_____the pot.

Write the missing words in the spaces below:

ONE	MORE THAN ONE
friend	_____
recipe	_____
pound	_____
piece	_____
carrot	_____
potato	_____
onion	_____
minute	_____

Use all the above words in the sentences below:

1. Mrs. Mara is my good_____.

2. I gave my_____to my friend.

3. I buy one_____of beef.

4. I buy the meat in one_____.

5. I cut one_____.

6. I cut one_____.

7. I use one_____.

8. I will cook the meat in one _____.

1. I have many_____.

2. I give_____to my friends.

3. I got two_____of beef.

4. I cut the meat into_____.

5. I cut many_____.

6. I cut several_____.

7. I use several_____.

8. I cook the stew for thirty _____.

40

Make your own sentences using these words:

boil

cut

drain

cover

recipe

add

carrots

teaspoon

slowly

sliced

1. _____
   _____ .

2. _____
   _____ .

3. _____
   _____ .

4. _____
   _____ .

5. _____
   _____ .

6. _____
   _____ .

7. _____
   _____ .

8. _____
   _____ .

9. _____
   _____ .

10. _____
    _____ .

Build new words:

ew	ook
d e w	b o o k
f_____	c_____
p_____	h_____
s_____	l_____
	t_____

all	ice
b a l l	d i c e
c_____	l_____
f_____	m_____
h_____	n_____
m_____	r_____
t_____	v_____
w_____	

42

Write these words in the spaces:

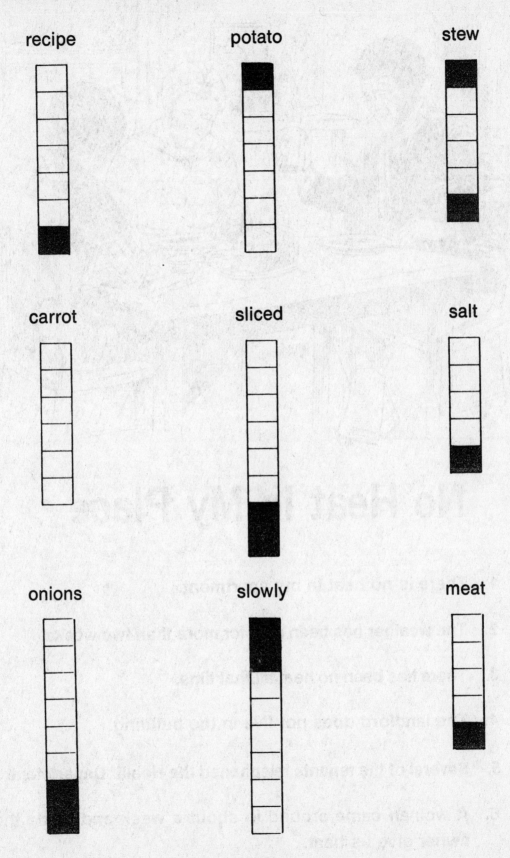

recipe

potato

stew

carrot

sliced

salt

onions

slowly

meat

43

No Heat In My Place

1. There is no heat in my apartment.

2. The weather has been cold for more than two weeks.

3. There has been no heat all that time.

4. The landlord does not live in the building.

5. Several of the tenants telephoned the Health Department.

6. A woman came around in about a week and made the owner give us heat.

Use one of these words in these sentences:

owner

apartment

heat

weather

weeks

time

landlord

around

woman

tenants

telephoned

There is no_____in my_____.

The _____has been cold for more than two weeks.

There has been no_____all that time.

The_____does not live in the building.

Several of the_____telephoned the Health Department.

A_____came around in about a week and made the_____give us heat.

Write the missing words in the spaces below:

NOW	YESTERDAY
_____	was
_____	did
_____	lived
_____	telephoned
_____	came
_____	made
_____	gave

Use all the above words in the sentences below:

1. This_____my home.

1. The weather_____cold last week.

2. I_____my best for my family.

2. I_____my best for my family.

3. I_____in this house.

3. We_____here for a year.

4. I_____my friend.

4. My friend_____me.

5. Please_____and eat dinner with me.

5. My friends_____to dinner.

6. I_____a cake.

6. I_____a cake for you.

7. I_____my name and address to the landlord.

7. I_____the landlord my name and address.

46

Write the missing words in the spaces below:

ONE	MORE THAN ONE
apartment	_____
week	_____
landlord	_____
owner	_____
tenant	_____
woman	_____
department	_____

Use all the above words in the sentences below:

1. My_____has no heat.

2. There was no heat for a _____.

3. One_____we had heat.

4. The_____does not live here.

5. I have been a_____for one year.

6. A _____came to see the building.

7. The Health_____helped us.

1. Many_____have no heat.

2. There was no heat for many _____.

3. Many_____we have no heat.

4. Many_____are not around.

5. Many_____do not have heat.

6. Two _____came to see the building.

7. There are many_____in the building.

47

Use one of these words in these sentences:

apartment

heat

about

landlord

weeks

time

weather

tenants

telephoned

winter

1. He has no_____in his place.

2. I have lived in my_____for two years.

3. The_____does not live here.

4. I have not seen the owner for_____.

5. I have lived here for some_____.

6. The_____has been cold all winter.

7. My apartment has been cold all_____.

8. All the_____have no heat in their places.

9. We_____the health department.

10. The_____is not around today.

Build new words:

ore

b o r e ____

c _____

m _____

p _____

s _____

t _____

w _____

ive

d i v e ____

h _____

l _____

ace

f a c e ____

l _____

m _____

p _____

r _____

ame

c a m e ____

f _____

g _____

l _____

s _____

t _____

Write these words in the spaces:

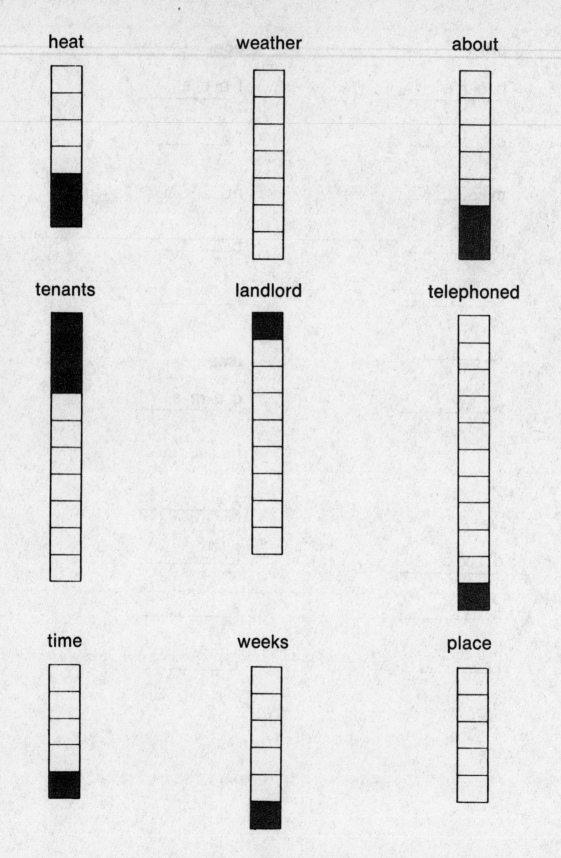

heat

weather

about

tenants

landlord

telephoned

time

weeks

place

I Like Baseball

1. I like to watch a baseball game on TV.

2. Sometimes I buy a ticket to a ball game.

3. Sometimes my boss gives me a free ticket to the game.

4. I know the names of most of the ball players.

5. I like to take the subway to the ball park.

6. I like spending an afternoon at the ball park.

7. My team has a good chance to win the pennant next year.

Use one of these words in these sentences:

baseball

game

sometimes

players

batting average

team

chance

win

pennant

subway

spending

I like to watch a_____game on TV.

Sometimes I buy a_____to a ball game.

_____my boss gives me a free ticket to a game.

I know the names of most of the_____.

I take the_____to the ball park.

I like_____an afternoon at the ball park.

My team has a good chance to win the_____ next year.

Write the missing words in the spaces below:

NOW	YESTERDAY
like	_____
watch	_____
buy	_____
give	_____
know	_____
is	_____
have	_____
win	_____

Use all the above words in the sentences below:

1. I_____to watch a ball game.

2. We_____the game on TV.

3. I do not_____tickets to the game.

4. I_____my boss a ticket some-times.

5. I_____the names of the players.

6. This_____a good ball game.

7. I_____a good time at the ball park.

8. I hope my team can_____the pennant.

1. We_____the last game.

2. We_____two games.

3. My boss_____tickets.

4. My boss_____me a ticket last week.

5. Last year I_____the names of the players.

6. It_____a good game.

7. I_____fun at the ball park.

8. My team_____the pennant last year.

53

Write the missing words in the spaces below:

ONE	MORE THAN ONE
_____	games
_____	tickets
_____	bosses
_____	players
_____	subways
_____	teams
_____	pennants
_____	years

Use all the above words in the sentences below:

1. I went to one ball_____.

2. My boss gave me a_____.

3. My_____often gives me a ticket.

4. I have a favorite_____.

5. I ride the_____.

6. I have a favorite baseball _____.

7. My team won a_____last year.

8. I hope my team wins the pennant this_____.

1. I saw ten_____last year.

2. My boss buys_____to the game every year.

3. Many_____give tickets to their men.

4. I know the names of the _____.

5. The_____are easy to ride.

6. There are many ball _____.

7. Some teams have won several _____.

8. I have watched my team for several_____.

Build new words:

atch

b a t c h

c_____

h_____

l_____

m_____

p_____

age

p a g e

r_____

s_____

w_____

eam

b e a m

r_____

s_____

t_____

ood

f o o d

g_____

h_____

m_____

st_____

w_____

Write one of these words in these sentences:

names

year

baseball

pennant

game

win

ticket

sometimes

chance

players

1. I like to watch_____.

2. I watched the_____yesterday.

3. My boss gave me a_____to the ball game.

4. _____I watch two games.

5. I know the_____of many of the players.

6. There are many ball_____.

7. My team has a_____to win.

8. My team will_____this year.

9. My team will win the_____.

10. This a good_____for my team.

Write these words in the spaces:

ticket   batting   players

baseball   favorite   averages

watch   game   teams

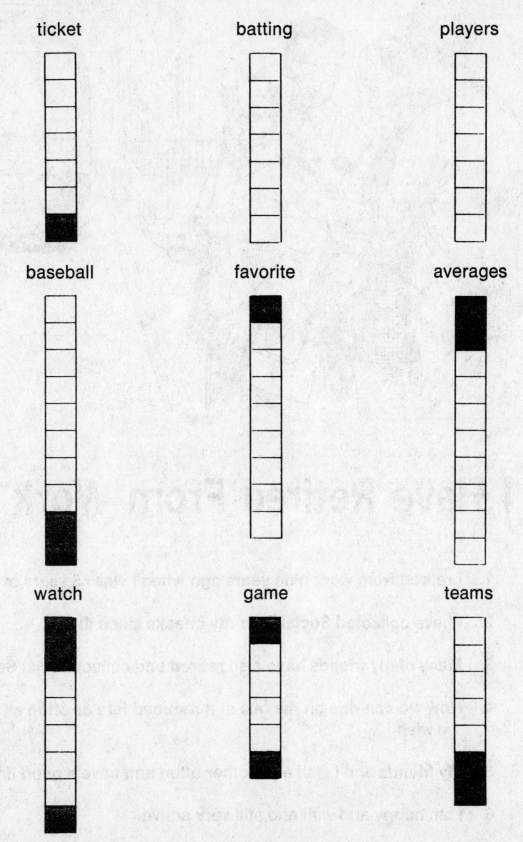

I Have Retired From Work

1. I retired from work nine years ago when I was 65 years of age.

2. I have collected Social Security checks since then.

3. Many of my friends have also retired and collect Social Security.

4. Now we can ride on the bus at a reduced fare as often as we wish.

5. My friends and I visit each other often and have a good time.

6. I am happy and well and still very active.

Use one of these words in these sentences:

retired

friends

ago

age

Social Security

collected

active

fare

reduced

I_____from work nine years ago when I was 65 years of age.

I have_____Social Security checks since then.

Many of my_____have also retired and collect Social Security.

Now we can ride on the bus at a_____fare as often as we wish.

My_____and I see each other often and have a good time.

I am happy and well and still very_____.

Write the missing words in the spaces below:

NOW	YESTERDAY
_____	had
_____	was
_____	retired
_____	collected
_____	rode
_____	visited

Use all the above words in the sentences below:

1. I_____several friends.

2. I_____still active.

3. My friend can_____at age 65.

4. I_____Social Security.

5. I can_____at a reduced fare.

6. I like to_____friends.

1. I_____many friends.

2. I_____active last year.

3. I_____at age 65.

4. I_____Social Security last year.

5. I_____on the bus yesterday.

6. My friends_____me yesterday.

Write the missing words in the spaces below:

ONE	MORE THAN ONE
year	_____
check	_____
bus	_____
fare	_____
friend	_____
time	_____

Use all the above words in the sentences below:

1. Last_____I was very well.

1. I went to work for several _____.

2. I got my Social Security _____.

2. I get many_____from them.

3. I ride on the_____for a reduced fare.

3. I ride on many_____.

4. The_____is reduced for me.

4. The bus_____are reduced.

5. I ride on the bus to visit my _____.

5. I visit my_____.

6. We had a good_____ together.

6. We have many good _____.

61

Build new words:

ide

h i d e

r_____

s_____

t_____

w_____

an

b a n

c_____

f_____

m_____

p_____

t_____

ong

l o n g

g_____

s_____

ill

b i l l

f_____

g_____

h_____

k_____

m_____

p_____

s_____

t_____

w_____

62

Use one of these words in these sentences:

retire

still

active

reduced

age

ago

fare

collect

together

1. I will_____at age 65.

2. I will be 65 years of_____.

3. I will_____Social Security checks.

4. I can ride on the bus at a_____fare.

5. My friend retired several years_____.

6. I can ride on the bus at a reduced_____.

7. My friends and I have good times_____.

8. I am_____very active.

9. I keep very_____.

Write these words in the spaces:

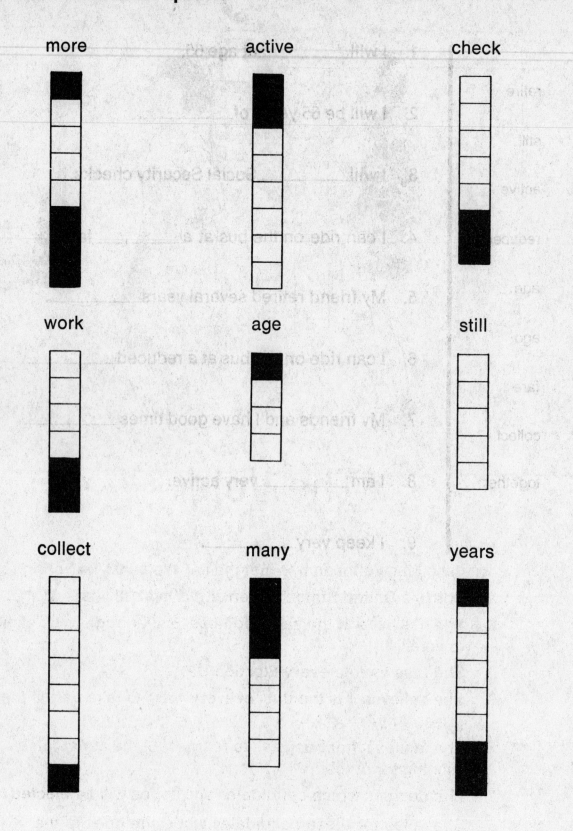

more   active   check

work   age   still

collect   many   years

The Voter

1. Lillie Mae Johnson has met the requirements for voting.

2. She is a United States citizen and is over 18 years of age.

3. She has lived at the same address long enough to be eligible to vote.

4. She tries to vote every Election Day.

5. She believes it is the duty of every voter to take part in the government.

6. She makes it her business to read about the candidates running for office.

7. She decides which candidates she hopes will be elected.

8. She votes for these candidates when she goes to the polling place on Election Day.

Use one of these words in these sentences:

requirements

voting

enough

citizen

eligible

believes

duty

government

business

candidates

running

office

polling place

Election Day

Lillie Mae Johnson has met the_____for voting.

She is a United States_____and is over 18 years of age.

She has lived at the same address long enough to be_____to vote.

She tries to vote on every_____.

She believes it is the duty of every voter to take part in the_____.

She makes it her_____to read about the candidates running for office.

She decides which_____she hopes will be elected.

She votes for these candidates when she goes to the_____on Election Day.

Write the missing words in the spaces below:

NOW	YESTERDAY
meet	_____
live	_____
vote	_____
believe	_____
make	_____
read	_____
run	_____
decide	_____

Use all the above words in the sentences below:

1. I can_____the requirements for voting.

2. I_____near the polling place.

3. I_____every Election Day.

4. I_____citizens should vote.

5. I_____it my business to vote.

6. I_____the newspaper every day.

7. Many persons_____for office.

8. I_____which candidates I want.

1. My husband_____the requirements last year.

2. We_____there many years.

3. My friends_____on Election Day.

4. I_____my friends voted.

5. I_____it my business to vote.

6. Yesterday I_____the newspaper.

7. Ten women_____for office.

8. I_____which candidate I wanted to win.

Write the missing words in the spaces below:

ONE	MORE THAN ONE
_____	requirements
_____	citizens
_____	duties
_____	candidates
_____	offices
_____	polling places

Use all the above words in the sentences below:

1. One_____for voting is to be a U.S. citizen.

2. Only a_____can vote.

3. I have a_____as a citizen.

4. I vote for my favorite_____.

5. I know who is running for _____.

6. I vote at my_____every year.

1. There are other_____for voting.

2. Only_____can vote.

3. We all have many_____.

4. Many_____run for office.

5. Many_____have many candidates.

6. _____are open all day.

Write the missing words in the spaces below.

TODAY	TOMORROW
meets	_____
tries	_____
reads	_____
run	_____
believes	_____
votes	_____

1. She _____ the voter requirements now.

1. If she moves, she _____ not _____ the voting requirements.

2. She _____ to vote in all the elections.

2. She _____ to vote after work.

3. She _____ newspapers to learn about the candidates.

3. She _____ the newspaper later.

4. She could _____ for office herself.

4. Do you think she _____ for office?

5. She _____ in the government.

5. _____ she always _____ in the government?

6. She _____ several times a year.

6. She _____ tomorrow.

Use one of these words in these sentences:

requirements

polling place

voting

citizen

enough

office

eligible

candidates

government

believes

duty

1. I know the_____for voting.

2. I know the hours for_____.

3. I have_____time to vote now.

4. I am a_____of the United States.

5. I am_____to vote.

6. She_____it is her duty to vote.

7. I believe it is my_____to vote.

8. We elect candidates to run the_____.

9. It is the_____of citizens to vote.

10. Many_____run for office.

11. Many candidates run for_____.

12. I live near a_____.

70

Build new words:

art

c a r t _____

d_____

m_____

p_____

t_____

w_____

ake

b a k e _____

c_____

f_____

l_____

m_____

r_____

s_____

t_____

w_____

Make words from these:

v t e o _____

d y u t _____

s c a n d i d t e a _____

c i d e d e _____

Write these words in the spaces:

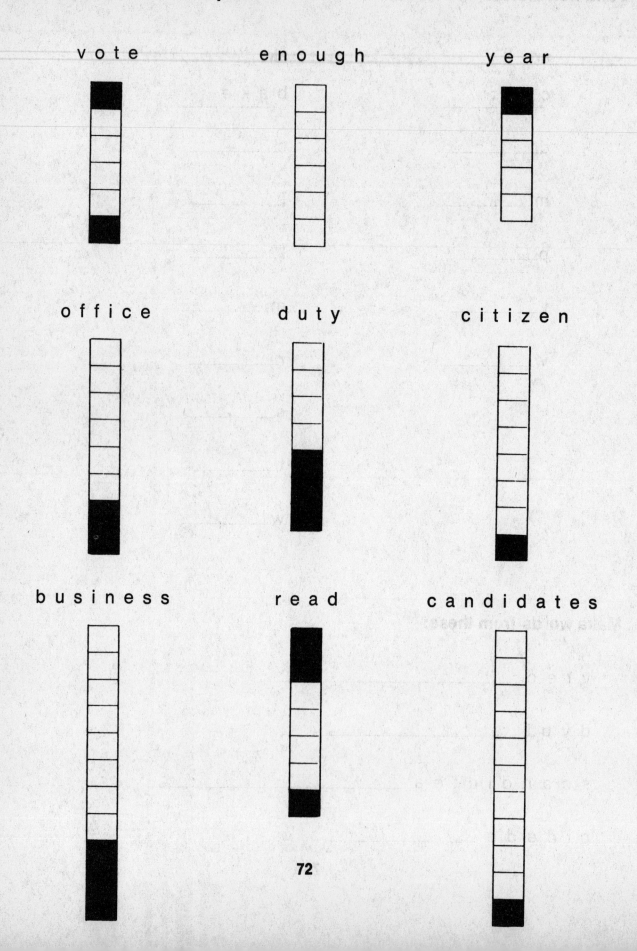

vote   enough   year

office   duty   citizen

business   read   candidates

Fill in the missing words.

ONE	MORE THAN ONE
1. recipe	_____
2. ball player	_____
3. _____	teaspoons
4. place	_____
5. _____	carrots
6. week	_____
7. owner	_____
8. department	_____
9. _____	buses
10. requirement	_____

NOW	TOMORROW
1. retire	_____
2. _____	will give
3. am	_____
4. _____	will win
5. watch	_____
6. _____	will know
7. _____	will collect
8. see	_____
9. visit	_____
10. believe	_____

Check the words you know:

____recipe
____stew meat
____potatoes
____peeled
____carrots
____sliced
____onions
____drain
____teaspoon
____add
____salt
____pepper
____slowly
____cover
____heat
____place
____weather
____weeks
____time
____landlord
____around
____tenants
____telephoned
____Health Department
____about
____baseball
____game

____ticket
____sometimes
____ball players
____team
____chance
____pennant
____retired
____ago
____age
____Social Security
____checks
____reduced
____fare
____together
____happy
____active
____requirements
____voter
____enough
____believes
____duty
____government
____business
____candidates
____running
____office
____polling place

These are the words you have learned in alphabetical order.
Check the ones you know.

a
___about
___active
___add
___age
___ago

b
___ball players
___baseball
___believes
___business

c
___candidates
___carrots
___chance
___checks
___cover

d
___drain
___duty

e
___Election Day
___eligible
___enough

f
___fare

g
___game
___government

h
___happy
___Health Department
___head

l
___landlord

o
___office
___onions

p
___peeled
___pennant
___pepper
___place
___polling place
___potatoes

r
___recipe
___reduced
___requirements
___retired
___running

s
___salt
___sliced
___slowly
___Social Security
___sometimes
___stew meat

t
___team
___teaspoon
___telephoned
___tenants
___ticket
___time
___together

v
___vote

w
___weather
___weeks

75

Practice

Build new words:

ook   **ong**

_____   _____

_____   _____

_____   _____

_____

ice   **ide**

_____   _____

_____   _____

_____   _____

_____

ace   **ill**

_____   _____

_____   _____

_____   _____

76

Practice

Write a word in each space in the sentences below:

1. My_____asked me to tell her how I make my stew.

2. I gave her this_____.

3. There is no_____in my place.

4. The_____does not live in the building.

5. I like to_____in elections.

6. His team has a good chance to win the_____this year.

7. I_____from work nine years ago.

8. I am happy and well and still very_____.

9. It is the_____of every citizen to vote on Election Day.

10. It is the duty of a_____to vote for_____ to public office.

Read The Ads Carefully

1. There are many kinds of ads in the newspapers every day.

2. Ads are meant to tell people what the stores have on sale.

3. Every word in an ad means something and should be read carefully.

4. Some ads are written to get people to spend money for items that are not a good buy for them.

5. Many people can be fooled by words in an ad that seem to promise good buys.

6. Most ads are honest and are not meant to fool the buyer.

Use one of these words in these sentences:

meant

ads

carefully

honest

buyer

promise

written

fooled

There are many kinds of _____ in the newspaper every day.

Ads are _____ to tell people what the stores have on sale.

Every word in an ad means something and should be read _____.

Some ads are _____ to get people to spend money for items that are not for them.

Many people can be _____ by words in an ad that seem to _____ good buys but are really not.

Most ads are _____ and are not meant to fool the _____.

79

Write the missing words in the spaces below.

NOW	YESTERDAY
_____	were
_____	meant
_____	had
_____	got
_____	spent
_____	fooled
_____	seemed
_____	promised
_____	did

Use all the words in the sentences below:

1. Coats_____on sale today.

2. The ads do not_____what they say.

3. I do not_____a newspaper now.

4. I_____a newspaper every day.

5. I like to_____an evening at home.

6. The words in ads do not _____me.

7. Most ads_____honest.

8. I_____the best I can.

1. Coats_____on sale yesterday.

2. The ad_____just what it said.

3. I_____a newspaper.

4. I_____a newspaper yesterday.

5. I_____the evening at home.

6. The words in the ad _____me.

7. The ads_____honest.

8. I_____what I promised.

80

Write the missing words in the spaces below.

ONE	MORE THAN ONE
kind	_____
newspaper	_____
ad	_____
word	_____
store	_____
sale	_____
item	_____
buyer	_____

Use all the words in the sentences below:

1. I like this_____of bread.

2. My_____has many ads in it.

3. I read each_____carefully.

4. I read every_____in the ads.

5. One_____had six ads.

6. I read about a_____of coats.

7. The price of each_____was in the ad.

1. There are many _____of breads.

2. There are two_____in my city.

3. There are many_____in the newspapers.

4. I read all of the_____in each ad.

5. Many _____put ads in the newspapers.

6. I read about many_____.

7. Many_____are on sale.

81

Build new words:

ord

c o r d _____

l_____

f_____

ean

b e a n _____

l_____

m_____

w_____

ool

f o o l _____

p_____

t_____

w_____

est

b e s t _____

n_____

p_____

r_____

t_____

w_____

First, write the missing word in each sentence. Then make your own sentence using the same word.

ads

carefully

items

honest

word

1. I like to read the_____every day.

_____

2. I read each_____carefully.

_____

3. I read every word_____.

_____

4. Most ads are_____.

_____

5. Many_____are on sale in the stores.

_____

Write these words in the spaces:

written   ad   honest   promise

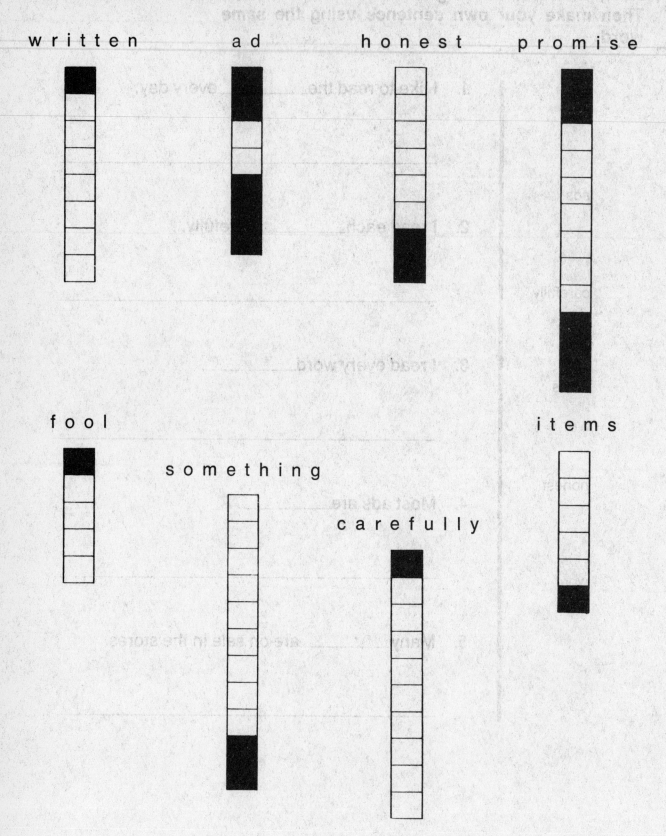

fool

something

carefully

items

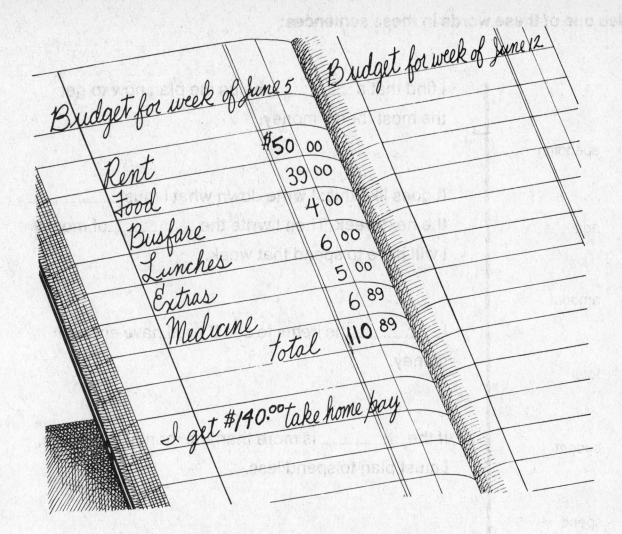

Budget for week of June 5

	$50	00
Rent	39	00
Food	4	00
Busfare	6	00
Lunches	5	00
Extras	6	89
Medicine		
total	110	89

I get $140.00 take home pay

Budget for week of June 12

I Have A Budget

1. I find that a budget helps me plan how to get the most for my money.

2. It goes like this: I write down what I must spend the next week.

3. Then I write the amount of money I will have to spend that week.

4. I add the items to see if I will have enough money.

5. If the total is more than the money I will have, I must plan to spend less.

6. If the total is less than the money I will have, the budget is good.

7. This way I can see where my money goes each week.

8. I can tell if I am spending too much money for any one item.

Use one of these words in these sentences:

spending

add

amount

total

budget

spend

less

money

I find that a _____ helps me plan how to get the most for my money.

It goes like this: I write down what I must _____ the next week. Then I write the _____ of money I will have to spend that week.

I _____ the items to see if I will have enough money.

If the _____ is more than the money I will have, I must plan to spend less.

If the total is _____ than the money I will have, the budget is good.

This way I can see where my _____ goes each week.

I can tell if I am _____ too much money for any one item.

Write the missing words in the spaces below.

NOW	YESTERDAY
_____	found
_____	helped
_____	planned
_____	got
_____	wrote
spend	_____
add	_____
see	_____
go (goes)	_____

Use all the words in the sentences below:

1. I_____a budget_____me.

2. I_____to use a budget.

3. I_____a chance to see where my money_____.

4. I_____down what I_____.

5. I_____the items.

6. I _____that I spend too much.

7. I can tell where my money _____.

1. I_____a budget_____ me.

2. I_____to use a budget.

3. I_____a chance to see where my money_____.

4. I_____down what I_____.

5. I_____all the items.

6. I _____that I spent too much.

7. I could tell where my money _____.

Write the missing words in the spaces below.

ONE	MORE THAN ONE
budget	_____
week	_____
amount	_____
item	_____
total	_____

Use all the words in the sentences below:

1. I want to keep a_____.

2. This_____I did not save any money.

3. I do not save a large_____ of money.

4. I will take out one_____ from my budget.

5. The_____budget is too much.

1. _____help people.

2. Two_____ago I saved some money.

3. The budget saves large _____of money.

4. Some_____cost a lot.

5. The_____of my budgets are less than the money I make.

88

Use one of these words in these sentences:

budget

spend

item

plan

amount

1. I will try to make a_____to help save money.

2. I_____to work on my budget today.

3. I write the_____of money I spend.

4. Each_____in the budget is listed.

5. I_____the total budget.

Make words from these:

b e t d g u _____

e m t i _____

l a t o t _____

m u t a o n _____

Write these words in the spaces:

budget

spending

money

plan

amount

item

total

spend

told

Willie Drives A Cab

1. Willie drives a cab for a fleet owner.

2. He usually works a night shift.

3. Sometimes he changes with another driver and works the day shift.

4. Willie wanted to find out on which shift he could make the most money.

5. After several months he decided that it really made little difference.

6. The amount of money he got depended upon how alert he was and how hard he worked.

7. His boss was a good fellow and let Willie choose the shift he wanted.

8. Willie chose the day shift so he could spend more time with his family and friends.

Use one of these words in these sentences:

fleet owner

usually

shift

changes

decided

difference

depended

alert

choose

chose

1. Willie drives a cab for a_____.

2. He_____works a night shift.

3. Sometimes he_____with another driver and works the day shift.

4. Willie wanted to find out on which_____he could make the most money.

5. After several months he_____that it really made little_____.

6. The amount of money_____upon how _____he was and how hard he worked.

7. His boss was a good fellow and let Willie _____the shift he wanted.

8. Willie_____the day_____so he could spend more time with his family and friends.

Write the missing words in the spaces below.

NOW	YESTERDAY
_____	drove
_____	worked
_____	changed
_____	wanted
_____	made
_____	got
_____	depended
_____	let
_____	chose
_____	spent

Use all the words on page 93 in the sentences below:

NOW	**YESTERDAY**
1. I_____a cab.	1. I_____a cab yesterday.
2. I_____a day shift.	2. I_____the night shift.
3. I want to_____my shift.	3. I_____my shift.
4. I do not_____to work days.	4. I_____to work nights.
5. I_____more money at night.	5. I_____less money at night.
6. I hope I_____the shift I _____.	6. I_____the shift I_____.
7. It_____upon the boss.	7. It_____upon the boss.
8. He_____me choose my shift.	8. He_____me take the night shift.
9. I want to_____my shift.	9. I_____the night shift.
10. I can_____more time with my friends.	10. I_____more time with my friends.

94

Write the missing words in the spaces below:

ONE	MORE THAN ONE
cab	_____
fleet	_____
owner	_____
shift	_____
driver	_____
month	_____
boss	_____
time	_____
family	_____
friend	_____

95

Use all the words on page 95 in the sentences below:

ONE	MORE THAN ONE
1. I drive a_____.	1. My friends drive_____.
2. The owner has a_____of cabs.	2. My boss has two_____.
3. The_____has a fleet of cabs.	3. Some owners have two _____.
4. I drive a day_____.	4. There are three_____.
5. I am a safe_____.	5. Many people are good _____.
6. My_____is good to me.	6. Most_____are good to the men.
7. I drove a cab for a_____.	7. Many_____I make good money.
8. At one_____I had a mean boss.	8. Many_____I make good _____.
9. I live with my_____.	9. Many _____ live in my building.
10. My_____drives a cab.	10. Many of my_____drive cabs.

Build new words:

i f t

d r i f t

g_____

l_____

r_____

s_____

i g h t

f i g h t

l_____

m_____

n_____

r_____

s_____

t_____

o s t

c o s t

h_____

l_____

m_____

p_____

e n d

b e n d

l_____

m_____

r_____

s_____

t_____

First, write the missing word in each sentence. Then make your own sentence using the same word.

fleet owner

usually

chose

boss

alert

1. My boss is the_____.

   _____.

2. I_____work the night shift.

   _____.

3. I keep_____and work hard.

   _____.

4. I_____not to work the day shift.

   _____.

5. I have a good_____.

   _____.

Make words from these:

s h o e c o _____

s t f h i _____

t r a e l _____

y e n o m _____

Write these words in the spaces:

choose   alert   fleet   depended

usually decided owner   shift

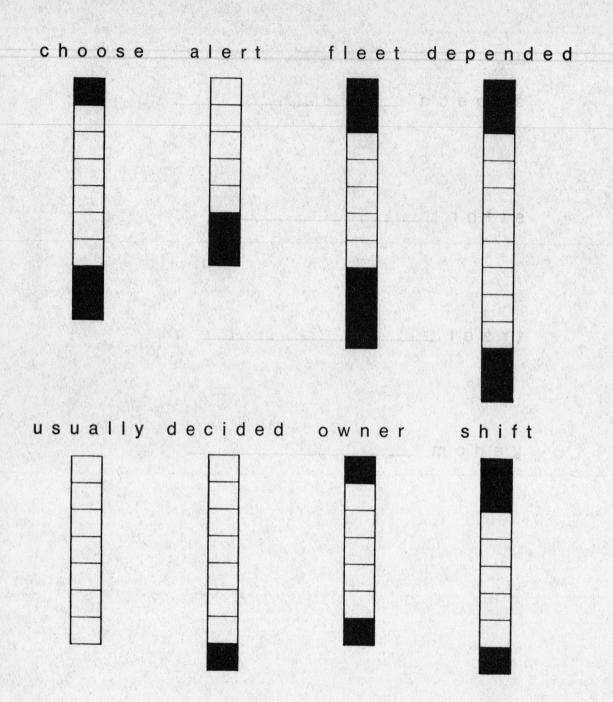

I Get A Vacation

1. The boss asked me when I wanted to take my vacation.

2. He asked me in March so he could arrange for someone to take over my work while I was away.

3. I had earned two weeks with pay during the year I had been with the company.

4. I decided to go in July and visit my mother.

5. I had not gone back home in four years and wanted to see my friends and relatives.

6. I had a good time in my home town and came back to the job feeling just great.

7. My friends and I spent a lot of time talking about our vacations.

Use these words in these sentences:

mother

talking

vacation

home town

arrange

March

earned

someone

company

pay

relatives

feeling

1. My boss asked me when I wanted to take my
    _____.

2. He asked me in_____so he could arrange
    for_____to take over my work while I was
    away.

3. I had _____ two weeks with _____ dur-
    ing the year I had been with the _____ .

4. I decided to go in July and visit my _____ .

5. I had not gone back home in four years, and I
    wanted to see my friends and _____ .

6. I had a good time in my_____and came
    back to the job_____just great.

7. My friends and I spent a lot of time_____
    about our vacations.

Write the missing words in the spaces below.

NOW	YESTERDAY
ask	_____
want	_____
take	_____
arrange	_____
earn	_____
decide	_____
see	_____
have	_____
come	_____
feel	_____
spend	_____
talk	_____

103

Use all the words on page 103 in the sentences below:

NOW

1. I_____my friend to go with me.

2. I_____to take a vacation.

3. I want to_____a vacation.

4. I want to_____a nice trip.

5. I want to_____more money.

6. I will_____where to go.

7. I want to_____my mother.

8. I _____two weeks of va-cation.

9. I want you to_____with me.

10. I_____just great.

11. I_____too much money.

12. I like to_____with my friends.

YESTERDAY

1. My friend_____me to go.

2. I _____to go to my home town.

3. I _____two weeks off.

4. I _____a trip.

5. I_____more money today.

6. I_____to go to my home town.

7. I _____my mother.

8. I _____a good time.

9. My friend_____with me.

10. I_____great after my vacation.

11. I _____too much money.

12. I_____with many friends while I was away.

Write the missing words in the spaces below.

ONE	MORE THAN ONE
vacation	_____
boss	_____
week	_____
year	_____
company	_____
mother	_____
relative	_____
friend	_____
time	_____
home town	_____

Use all the words on page 105 in the sentences below:

ONE

1. I had a good_____.

2. My _____is a good person.

3. I must work this_____.

4. This_____I got a vacation.

5. I work for a good_____.

6. My _____ lives far away.

7. I have one _____ in my home town.

8. My_____works in my company.

9. I do not have much_____ to rest.

10. I like visiting my _____.

MORE THAN ONE

1. _____are good for me.

2. Most _____ are good persons.

3. The next two_____I am off.

4. For two_____I had no vacation.

5. Most_____give vacations.

6. _____like to see their children.

7. My_____do not live here.

8. I have several_____who work with me.

9. I have good_____with my friends.

10. Most people like to go back to visit their _____.

Build new words:

ay

b a y

d_____

g_____

h_____

l_____

m_____

p_____

r_____

s_____

ear

b e a r

g_____

h_____

n_____

p_____

r_____

y_____

t_____

d_____

ust

b u s t

d_____

g_____

j_____

l_____

m_____

r_____

eat

b e a t

f_____

h_____

m_____

n_____

p_____

s_____

Make words from these:

g a r a r e n _____

c t v a i a n o _____

y n p a m o c_____

s e n o m e o _____

d r e n a e _____

First, write the missing word in each sentence. Then make your own sentence using the same word.

vacation

March

arrange

company

feeling

talking

1. I had a good time on my_____.

   _____.

2. I work for a good_____.

   _____.

3. I came home_____just great.

   _____.

4. I want to go away in_____.

   _____.

5. I spent time_____with my friends.

   _____.

6. I can_____a vacation.

   _____.

Write these words in the spaces:

arrange   March   earned   someone

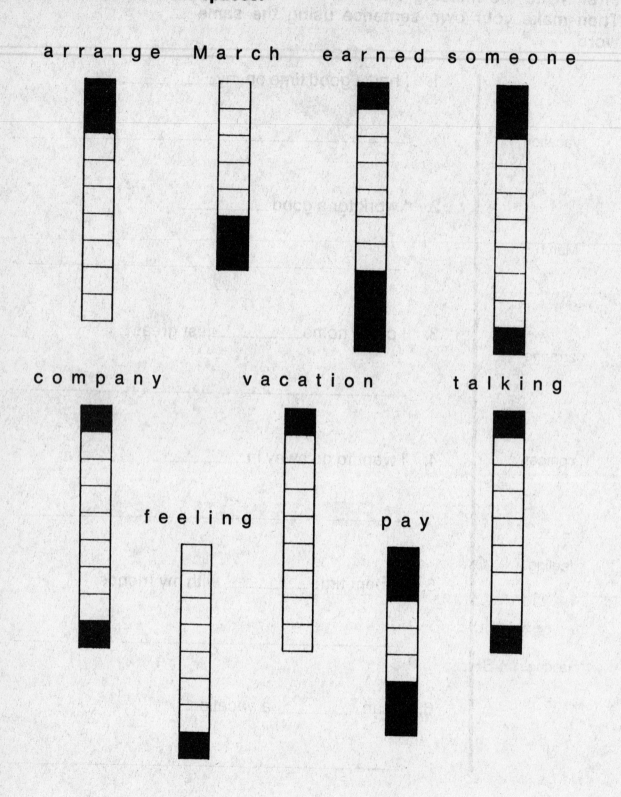

company   vacation   talking

feeling   pay

110

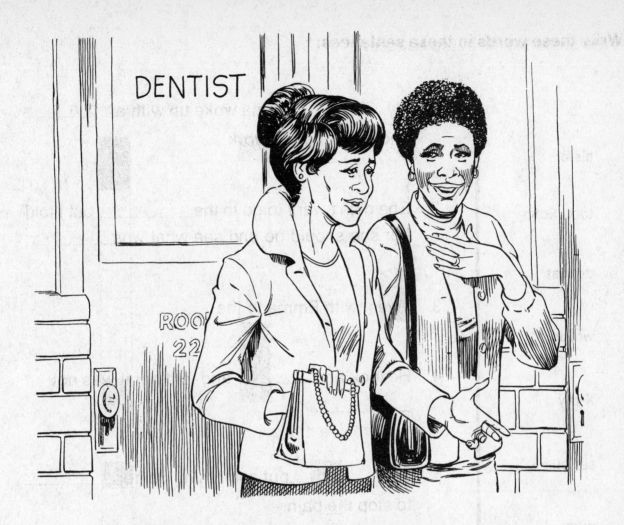

Emma Had A Toothache

1. My sister Emma woke up with a toothache and did not go to work.

2. She didn't want to go to the dentist, but I told
her she should go and see what was wrong.

3. I went with Emma to the dentist.

4. He took an X-ray of the tooth and told her it was not serious.

5. The dentist put something on her gum to stop the pain.

6. He gave her some tablets to take if the pain came back.

7. When we got home, Emma said she was glad
I had made her go to the dentist.

Write these words in these sentences:

sister

toothache

dentist

wrong

X-ray

serious

gum

pain

tablets

1. My_____Emma woke up with a_____ and did not go to work.

2. She didn't want to go to the_____, but I told her she should go and see what was_____.

3. I went with Emma to the_____.

4. He took an_____and told her it was not _____.

5. The_____put something on her_____ to stop the pain.

6. He gave her some_____to take if the _____came back.

7. When we got home, Emma said she was glad I had made her go to the_____.

Write the missing words in the spaces below.

NOW	YESTERDAY
wake	_____
go	_____
want	_____
tell	_____
see	_____
take	_____
is	_____
put	_____
stop	_____
come	_____
get	_____
say	_____
make	_____

113

Use all the words on page 113 in the sentences below:

NOW	YESTERDAY
1. I_____up early.	1. I_____up early.
2. I_____to work early.	2. I_____to work early.
3. I_____to earn money.	3. I_____to buy a car.
4. _____me your name.	4. I_____you my name.
5. I_____what you mean.	5. I_____the dentist.
6. I _____Emma to work.	6. I _____Emma to see the dentist.
7. He_____not far from my house.	7. He_____three blocks away.
8. He_____something on my gum.	8. He_____something on my gum.
9. I can _____to talk with you today.	9. I_____at the store to buy some food.
10. _____with me to the dentist.	10. I_____home later.
11. I_____up early.	11. I_____up late today.
12. What did you_____?	12. I_____goodbye.
13. I can_____a cake every week.	13. I_____a cake yesterday.

114

Write the missing words in the spaces below.

ONE	MORE THAN ONE
sister	_____
toothache	_____
dentist	_____
X-ray	_____
tooth	_____
gum	_____
tablet	_____
home	_____

Use all the words in the sentences below:

1. I have a_____.

2. I have a_____.

3. I have a good_____.

4. He took an_____of my tooth.

5. I have one_____that aches.

6. My_____is sore.

7. I took a_____for my toothache.

8. I went_____after work.

1. My friend has three_____.

2. _____always hurt a lot.

3. Three _____live in my building.

4. He took three_____.

5. I have two_____that ache.

6. My_____are sore.

7. The dentist gave me some _____.

8. Many_____did not have heat this winter.

115

Build new words:

ook	op
b o o k	c o p
c_____	h_____
h_____	l_____
l_____	m_____
n_____	p_____
r_____	s_____
	t_____

um	et
b u m	b e t
g_____	g_____
h_____	j_____
pl_____	l_____
r_____	m_____
s_____	n_____
	p_____
	s_____
	w_____

116

Make words from these:

s t i n e d t _____

m g u _____

a n i p _____

g r o n w _____

117

First, write the missing word in each sentence. Then make your own sentence using the same word.

sister

dentist

serious

pain

tablets

1. My_____had a toothache.

   _____.

2. The_____took an X-ray.

   _____.

3. I had a lot of_____in my tooth.

   _____.

4. I took some_____for the pain.

   _____.

5. The dentist said there was nothing_____.

   _____.

Write these words in the spaces:

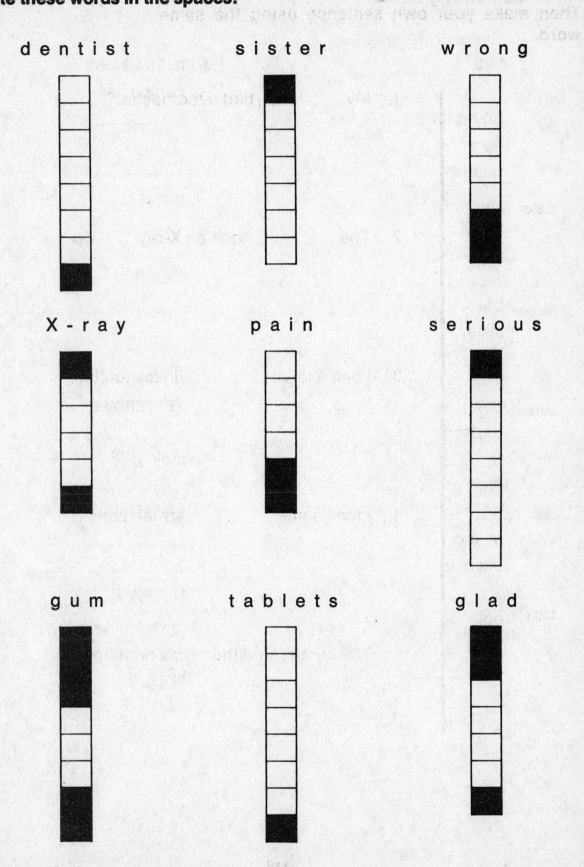

dentist

sister

wrong

X-ray

pain

serious

gum

tablets

glad

Fill in the missing words.

ONE	MORE THAN ONE
_____	companies
home town	_____
item	_____
budget	_____
_____	gums
tablet	_____
pain	_____
_____	friends
boss	_____
sister	_____

NOW	YESTERDAY
depend	_____
_____	took
earn	_____
_____	fooled
spend	_____
choose	_____
_____	changed
get	_____
is	_____
_____	gave

120

Check the words you know:

___advertisements	___depended
___ads	___alert
___carefully	___choose
___written	___chose
___items	___vacation
___fooled	___March
___promise	___arrange
___honest	___someone
___buyer	___earned
___budget	___pay
___spend	___company
___plan	___relatives
___amount	___home town
___add	___feeling
___total	___talking
___less	___sister
___money	___toothache
___spending	___dentist
___fleet owner	___wrong
___usually	___serious
___changed	___gum
___decided	___pain
___difference	___tablets
	___X-ray

**Here are the words you have learned in alphabetical order.
Check the ones you know.**

a
___add
___ads
___advertisements
___alert
___arrange

b
___budget
___buyer

c
___carefully
___changed
___choose
___chose
___company

d
___decided
___dentist
___depended
___difference

e
___earned

f
___feeling
___fleet owner
___fooled

g
___gum

h
___home town
___honest

i
___items

l
___less

m
___March
___money

p
___pain
___pay
___plan
___promise

r
___relatives

s
___serious
___sister
___someone
___spend
___spending

t
___tablets
___talking
___toothache
___total

u
___usually

v
___vacation

w
___written
___wrong

x
___X-ray

Practice

Make words from each of these:

ard

hard

_____

_____

_____

_____

eat

beat

_____

_____

_____

_____

ight

light

_____

_____

_____

_____

ong

song

_____

_____

_____

_____

ace

face

_____

_____

_____

_____

ust

just

_____

_____

_____

_____

ice

nice

_____

_____

_____

_____

ound

sound

_____

_____

_____

_____

eek

seek

_____

_____

_____

_____

Practice

Fill in the missing words in these sentences:

1. Some_____are written to get people to spend money for items that are not a good buy for them.

2. Most ads are_____and are not meant to fool the buyer.

3. I find that a_____helps me plan how to get the most for my money.

4. Willie drives a cab for a_____.

5. His_____was a good fellow and let Willie choose the_____ he wanted.

6. The_____asked me when I wanted to take my_____.

7. I had_____two weeks with pay for the four years I had been with the company.

8. My friends and I spent a lot of time talking about our_____.

9. My sister Emma woke up with a_____and did not go to work.

10. The_____put something on her gum to stop the_____.

I Get My Driver's License

Everyone who drives a car needs a driver's license. I need to drive to get to work.

First, I filled out the forms for a driver's license. Then I took tests to prove my ability. I took a written test to show that I knew the rules of driving. I took a driving test to show that I knew how to drive a car.

During the driving test, I had to drive on a busy street. I had to park correctly. I had to obey all the traffic rules.

I passed both tests. In a few weeks, my driver's license will be mailed to me.

Use one of these words in these sentences:

mailed

Everyone

written

forms

license

passed

driving

correctly

prove

drive

ability

1. _____who drives a car needs a driver's license.

2. First, I filled out the_____for a_____ license.

3. I took a_____test to show that I knew the rules of the road.

4. Then I took tests to_____my ability.

5. I took a_____test to show that I knew how to_____a car.

6. I had to park_____.

7. I_____both tests.

8. My driver's license was_____to me.

Write the missing words in the spaces below.

NOW	YESTERDAY
drive	_____
need	_____
fill	_____
take	_____
prove	_____
know	_____
park	_____
obey	_____
pass	_____
mail	_____

Use all the words in the sentences below:

1. I_____my car to work.
2. I_____a driver's license.
3. I _____out forms.
4. It did not_____very long.
5. I can_____I know how to drive a car.
6. I_____how to drive.
7. The examiner asks me to _____my driving.
8. I know how to_____a car.
9. I_____the traffic rules.
10. I can_____the driving tests.
11. They_____the license to me.

1. I_____my car to work.
2. I_____to get a license.
3. I _____out forms.
4. It_____a very long time.
5. I_____I knew how to drive.
6. I_____I had to take a test.
7. I_____how well I drove.
8. I_____the car for him.
9. I_____all the rules.
10. I_____the driving tests.
11. The license was_____to me.

127

Write the missing words in the spaces below.

ONE	MORE THAN ONE
license	_____
car	_____
week	_____
form	_____
I	_____
street	_____
test	_____
rule	_____

Use all the words in the sentences below:

1. I have a driver's_____.

2. I have an old_____.

3. I studied for the test for one _____.

4. I filled out a _____for my driver's license.

5. _____like to fill out forms.

6. I drove on one _____for my driver's test.

7. I must take a written_____.

8. I know the_____for stopping.

1. Many_____are issued.

2. All_____have licenses.

3. I spent several_____studying for the test.

4. When I became a citizen, I filled out several_____.

5. _____should all know how to fill out forms.

6. I drove on many _____when I took my driver's test.

7. I must take two_____.

8. I know all the traffic_____.

Make words from these:

s e l i c e n _____

f a r t i c f _____

o n e y v e r e _____

t r y o c r e c l _____

f r y l u t t h u l _____

d o b e y e _____

First, fill in the missing words. Then write your own sentences using the words.

driver's license

form

traffic

ability

passed

1. I wanted to get a_____ _____.

_____.

2. I_____all the tests for a driver's license.

_____.

3. I filled out a_____.

_____.

4. I drove in_____.

_____.

5. I knew I could prove my_____to drive.

_____.

Write these words in the spaces:

traffic   issued   rules   vehicle

license   obeyed   application

everyone   truthfully

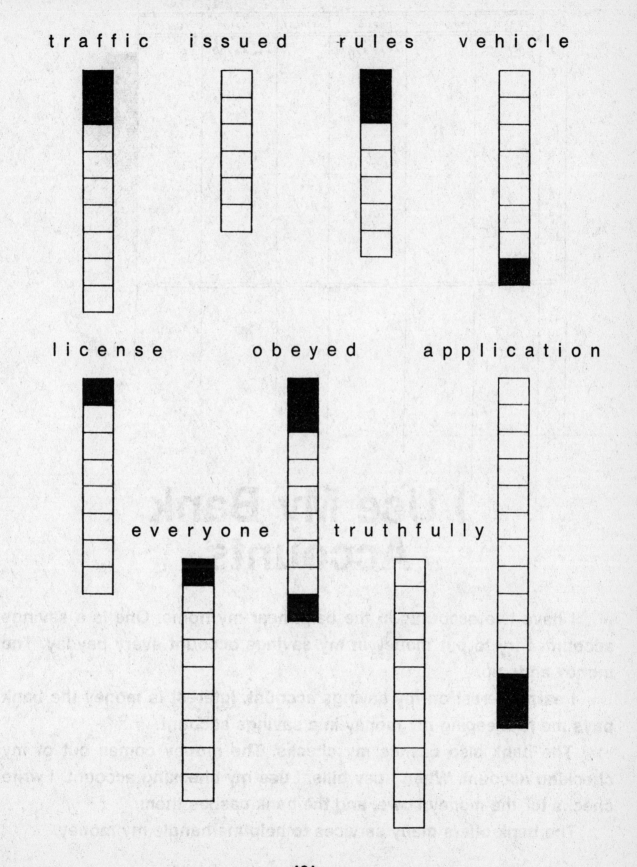

131

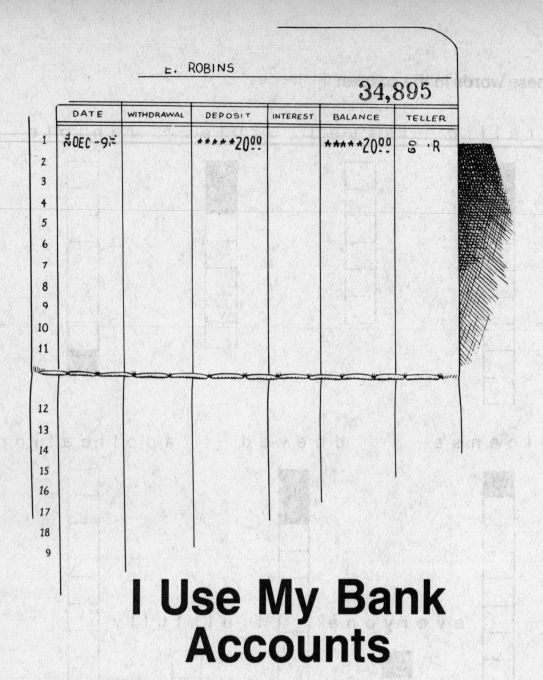

E. ROBINS

34,895

DATE	WITHDRAWAL	DEPOSIT	INTEREST	BALANCE	TELLER
1 20 DEC -9		****20.00		****20.00	G. R
2					
3					
4					
5					
6					
7					
8					
9					
10					
11					
12					
13					
14					
15					
16					
17					
18					
9					

I Use My Bank Accounts

I have two accounts in the bank near my home. One is a savings account. I try to put money in my savings account every payday. The money adds up.

I earn interest on my savings account. Interest is money the bank pays me for keeping my money in a savings account.

The bank also cashes my checks. The money comes out of my checking account. When I pay bills, I use my checking account. I write checks for the money I owe, and the bank cashes them.

The bank offers many services to help me handle my money.

Use one of these words in these sentences:

earn

accounts

services

account

payday

money

checks

interest

write

pay

cashes

savings

checking

I have two_____in the bank near my home. One is a _____account. I try to put money in my savings _____every _____. The _____adds up.

I _____interest on my savings account. _____is the money the bank pays me for keeping my_____in a savings account.

The bank also cashes my_____. The money comes out of my _____account. When I _____bills, I use my checking account. I _____checks for the money I owe, and the bank_____them.

The bank offers many_____to help me handle my money.

Write the missing words in the spaces below.

TODAY	YESTERDAY
have	_____
try	_____
earn	_____
cash	_____
use	_____
write	_____
owe	_____
adds	_____
pay	_____
comes	_____

Use the words on page 134 to fill in the missing spaces below.

NOW

1. I _____ learned how to save money.
2. I _____ to save $10 every payday.
3. I _____ interest on my savings account.
4. I _____ checks when I need money.
5. I _____ my checking account to pay bills.
6. I _____ checks to pay bills.
7. I _____ my friend $10.
8. The money in my savings accounts _____ up over a year.
9. I _____ my bills as soon as I can.
10. The money I save _____ out of my pay check.

YESTERDAY

1. I _____ to learn how to save money.
2. Last year, I _____ to save $8 every payday.
3. Last year, I _____ $40 on my savings account.
4. I _____ a check for $50 last week.
5. I _____ my savings account to save money.
6. I _____ six checks last month.
7. I _____ two payments on my car this year.
8. I _____ money to my savings account almost every week last year.
9. I _____ more for food last month.
10. Last year, some of the money I saved _____ from an income tax return.

Write the missing words in the spaces below.

ONE	MORE THAN ONE
bank	_____
account	_____
payday	_____
bill	_____
check	_____
I	_____
checking account	_____
service	_____
savings account	_____

Use the words on page 136 in these sentences.

ONE

1. I go to my_____every Friday.

2. My biggest _____is for checking.

3. _____is every Friday.

4. I pay one_____each payday.

5. I write a _____for every bill.

6. _____like saving money.

7. The money in my_____ _____goes down as I write checks.

8. My bank is a_____to me.

9. When I started working, I had one_____ _____.

MORE THAN ONE

1. I have accounts in two _____.

2. Bank_____are very convenient.

3. When I had two jobs, I had two _____.

4. Some persons pay their _____all at once.

5. I write about ten _____ a month.

6. _____should all try to save.

7. Married couples sometimes need two_____ _____.

8. My bank offers many _____.

9. Today, I have three _____ _____.

Make words from these:

t a c o n u c   _____

s t i n e r t e   _____

k i g n c h e c   _____

v i r e s e c s   _____

v s i n g a s   _____

o n m y e   _____

First, write the missing word in each sentence. Then make your own sentence using the same word.

account

interest

services

checking account

payday

earn

bank

1. I have two accounts in my_____.

   _____.

2. I earn_____on my savings account.

   _____.

3. I also have a checking_____.

   _____.

4. Every_____, I put money in my savings account.

   _____.

5. Do all banks provide the same_____?

   _____.

6. I think everyone needs a_____ _____.

   _____.

7. I like to_____money.

   _____.

Write these words in the spaces:

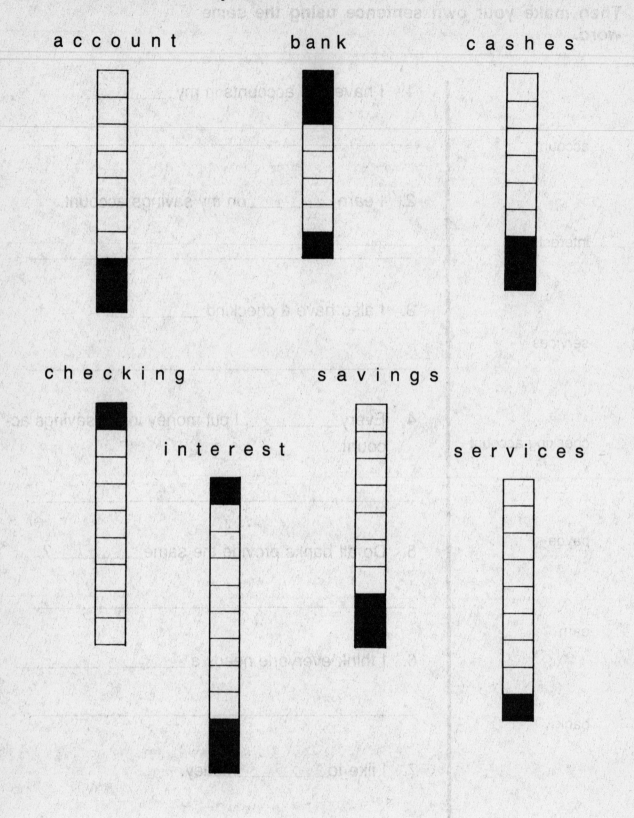

account

bank

cashes

checking

savings

interest

services

Paying Taxes

Everyone must file an income tax return with the federal government no matter how much money was received. The amount of tax you owe depends upon how much money you earned and how many deductions you have.

My only income is from my job, so I fill out the short form. It is easy to figure out how much I have to pay.

A friend runs a small business and also has a part-time job. He must use other forms that are harder to fill out. So he goes to the Internal Revenue office for help in filling out his forms. Anyone can go to a local office and get help with tax forms.

In some places, there are also state and city tax returns to fill out.

Use one of these words in these sentences:

local

forms

income tax return

figure

income

received

deductions

returns

federal

business

Everyone must file an _____ _____ _____ with the _____ government no matter how much money was _____. The amount of tax you owe depends upon how much money you earned and how many _____ you have.

My only _____ is from my job, so I fill out the short form. It is easy to _____ out how much I have to pay.

A friend runs a small _____ and also has a part-time job. He must use other forms that are harder to fill out. But he goes to the Internal Revenue Service for help in filling out his forms. Anyone can go to a _____ office and get help with tax _____.

In some places, there are also state and city tax _____ to fill out.

Write the missing words in the spaces below.

NOW		YESTERDAY
file		_____
pay		_____
depends		_____
use		_____
fill		_____
owe		_____
run		_____
figure		_____
mail		_____
receive		_____

Use all the words on page 143 in the sentences below:

NOW

1. I_____my federal tax return each year.

2. I must_____the entire amount.

3. I_____on my friend to help me.

4. I_____the short tax return form.

5. I_____in the items.

6. I do not_____much money.

7. I_____a small business.

8. I_____I owe a big tax this year.

9. I_____a check with my tax return.

YESTERDAY

1. I_____my federal tax return early.

2. I_____the entire amount.

3. I_____on him to help me.

4. I_____the long tax return last year.

5. I_____in my income tax return.

6. Last year I_____a lot of money.

7. I_____a small business last year.

8. My friend_____out my tax return for me.

9. My tax return was_____ yesterday.

Write the missing words in the spaces below.

ONE	MORE THAN ONE
tax return	_____
government	_____
amount	_____
person	_____
year	_____
job	_____
form	_____
friend	_____
business	_____
office	_____
state	_____

Use all the words on page 145 in the sentences below:

ONE

1. I mailed my_____.

2. The federal_____mails the tax form to me.

3. I figure the_____I owe.

4. Each_____must file a tax return.

5. The tax is paid every_____.

6. I have a new_____.

7. I file the federal tax_____.

8. I have a good_____.

9. I run a small_____.

10. I work in a big_____.

11. My_____does not have an income tax.

12. I work in a large_____.

MORE THAN ONE

1. I must file two_____.

2. Many_____are different from ours.

3. I think I owe several_____ of money.

4. All_____must file a tax return.

5. Some_____the tax is a large amount.

6. _____are not easy to find.

7. There are two federal income tax_____.

8. My_____are good to me.

9. Small_____are hard to run.

10. There are many_____in my building.

11. Some _____have in-come taxes.

12. I have lived in three_____.

146

Make words from these:

t o u n a m _____

s n u b i s e s _____

t r e n u r _____

f i c e f o _____

g r e i f u _____

d r e f l a e _____

t i y c _____

p r o n e s _____

t n e r g e v o m n _____

r a y e _____

First, write the missing word in each sentence. Then make your own sentence using the same word.

amount

1. I know the _____ of tax I owe.

   _____.

2. I worked in only one _____ last year.

   _____.

job

3. I fill out the short tax _____.

   _____.

form

4. I filled out my own _____ _____

   _____.

tax return

5. Filling out tax forms is my personal _____.

   _____.

business

6. My local tax _____ helps me with the forms.

   _____.

office

7. I pay taxes to the federal _____.

   _____.

government

state

8. Do you pay _____ taxes where you live?

   _____.

Write these words in the spaces:

a m o u n t   s t a t e   f r i e n d   b u s i n e s s

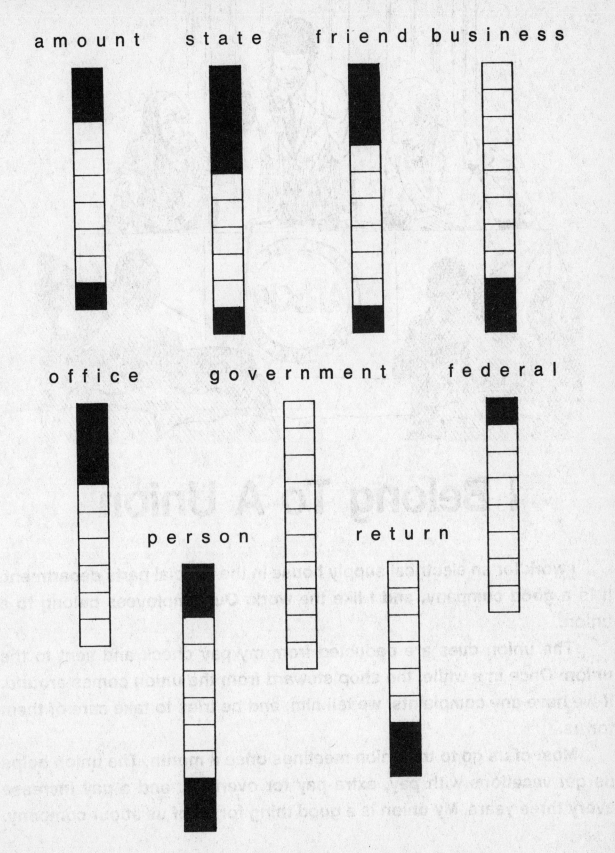

o f f i c e   g o v e r n m e n t   f e d e r a l

p e r s o n   r e t u r n

I Belong To A Union

I work for an electrical supply house in the special parts department. It is a good company, and I like the work. Our employees belong to a union.

The union dues are deducted from my pay check and sent to the union. Once in a while, the shop steward from the union comes around. If we have any complaints, we tell him, and he tries to take care of them for us.

Most of us go to the union meetings once a month. The union helps us get vacations with pay, extra pay for overtime, and a pay increase every three years. My union is a good thing for all of us at our company.

Use one of these words in these sentences:

union

electrical

special parts

employees

dues

deducted

shop steward

complaints

overtime

increase

I work for an_____supply house in the _____department. It is a good company and I like the work. Our_____belong to a_____ of people like myself.

The union _____are deducted from my pay check and sent to the_____. Once in a while the_____ _____ from the_____ comes around. If we have any_____ we tell him and he tries to take care of them for us.

Most of us go to the_____meetings once a month. The union helps us get vacations with pay, extra pay for_____and a pay_____every three years. My_____is a good thing for all of us at our company.

151

Write the missing words in the spaces below.

NOW	YESTERDAY
belong	_____
work	_____
like	_____
deduct	_____
send	_____
tell	_____
keep	_____
go	_____

Use all the words in the sentences below:

1. I_____to a union.

2. I_____five days a week.

3. I_____my job.

4. They_____union dues from my pay.

5. I_____money to my sister.

6. _____me where you live.

7. I try to_____well.

8. I_____to union meetings.

1. I have_____for two years.

2. I_____hard all week.

3. I_____my vacation last year.

4. Union dues were_____from my pay.

5. I_____her some money last week.

6. You_____me your address.

7. I_____well all last year.

8. I_____to the meeting last month.

Write the missing words in the spaces below.

ONE	MORE THAN ONE
_____	unions
_____	departments
_____	companies
_____	pay checks
_____	weeks
_____	stewards
_____	complaints
_____	increases
_____	meetings
	months

Use all the words on page 153 in the sentences below:

ONE	MORE THAN ONE
1. I belong to a_____.	1. There are many kinds of _____.
2. I work in a large_____.	2. My company has several _____.
3. My_____is good to me.	3. Many_____are good to their workers.
4. I get a_____ _____every week.	4. We get our_____ _____every week.
5. I get my pay check every _____.	5. I get two_____of vacation.
6. I know my shop_____.	6. Unions have shop_____.
7. I have no_____about my job.	7. We have no_____with our department.
8. I got an_____.	8. I did not get any_____this year.
9. I went to the union _____.	9. Union _____are held each month.
10. Each_____, I go to a union meeting.	10. Some_____, I go to two meetings.

Make words from these:

o n i n u _____

e d u s _____

t r e m e i v o _____

e m s l e o p y e _____

r a c e s i n e _____

First, write the missing word in each sentence. Then make your own sentence using the same word.

company

complaints

overtime

deducted

union

shop steward

sample

sent

1. I work for a good _____.

   _____.

2. I have very few _____.

   _____.

3. Sometimes I work and get paid for _____.

   _____.

4. Union dues are _____ from my pay check.

   _____.

5. I belong to a _____.

   _____.

6. I ask questions of the _____ _____.

   _____.

7. I showed a _____ of my work to my boss.

   _____.

8. I was _____ to work in another department.

   _____.

Write these words in the spaces:

union   special   company   deducted

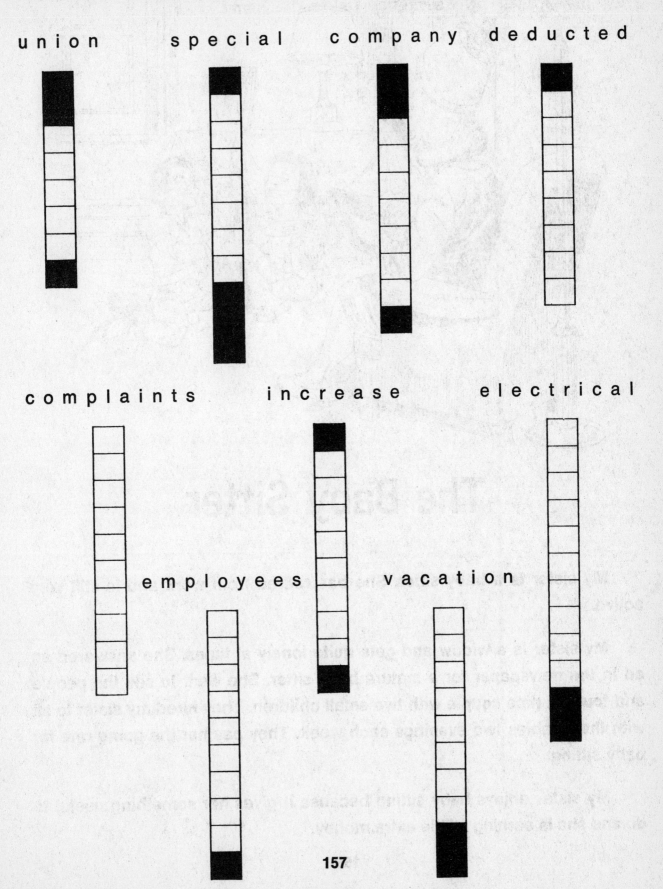

complaints   increase   electrical

employees   vacation

The Baby Sitter

My sister is a baby sitter. She has retired from work and is still very active.

My sister is a widow and gets quite lonely at times. She answered an ad in the newspaper for a mature baby sitter. She went to see the people and found a nice couple with two small children. They hired my sister to sit with their babies two evenings each week. They pay her the going rate for baby sitting.

My sister enjoys baby sitting because it gives her something useful to do and she is earning a little extra money.

Use these words in these sentences:

widow

useful

baby sitter

lonely

hired

answered

couple

mature

My sister is a _____. She has retired

from work and is still very active.

My sister is a_____and gets quite_____

at times. She_____an ad in the newspaper for a

_____baby sitter. She went to see the people

and found a nice_____with two small children.

They_____my sister to sit with their children two

evenings each week. They pay her the going rate

for baby sitting.

My sister enjoys baby sitting because it gives

her something_____to do and she is earning a

little extra money.

Write the missing words in the spaces below.

NOW	YESTERDAY
retire	_____
answer	_____
find	_____
hire	_____
sit	_____
pay	_____
enjoy	_____
earn	_____

Use all the words in the sentences below:

1. I am not ready to_____.

1. My friend_____last year.

2. I want to_____this ad.

2. I_____the ad for a baby sitter.

3. I_____the work easy.

3. He_____the work too hard.

4. I hope they will_____me.

4. I was_____as a baby sitter.

5. I_____down much of the time.

5. I_____down most of the day.

6. They _____me well.

6. They_____me for my work.

7. I_____being with children.

7. I_____my work with children.

8. I can_____some money.

8. I_____a little money.

Write the missing words in the spaces below.

ONE	MORE THAN ONE
sister	_____
baby sitter	_____
widow	_____
couple	_____
ad	_____
child	_____
baby	_____

Use all the words in the sentences below:

1. I have one_____.

2. I work as a_____.

3. My sister is a_____.

4. She answered an _____.

5. My sister works for a nice _____.

6. There is one _____in the family.

7. The couple also has one older_____.

1. My friend has three_____.

2. _____earn some money.

3. _____are good sitters.

4. There are many _____in the newspaper.

5. Many _____need a baby sitter.

6. There are two _____in the family.

7. Another couple has two older_____.

Make words from these:

d o w i w   _____

l e y l o n   _____

l e u s f u   _____

t r e m a u   _____

d r e h i   _____

d w a n e r s e   _____

c o l e u p   _____

First, write the missing word in each sentence. Then make your own sentence using the same word.

widow

lonely

mature

couple

hired

useful

1. My sister is a _____.

   _____.

2. Sometimes she feels a little _____.

   _____.

3. She is a _____ woman.

   _____.

4. A _____ I know is looking for a baby sitter.

   _____.

5. They _____ my sister.

   _____.

6. She is very _____ to them.

   _____.

Write these words in the spaces:

b a b y   s i t t e r   w i d o w   h i r e d   l o n e l y

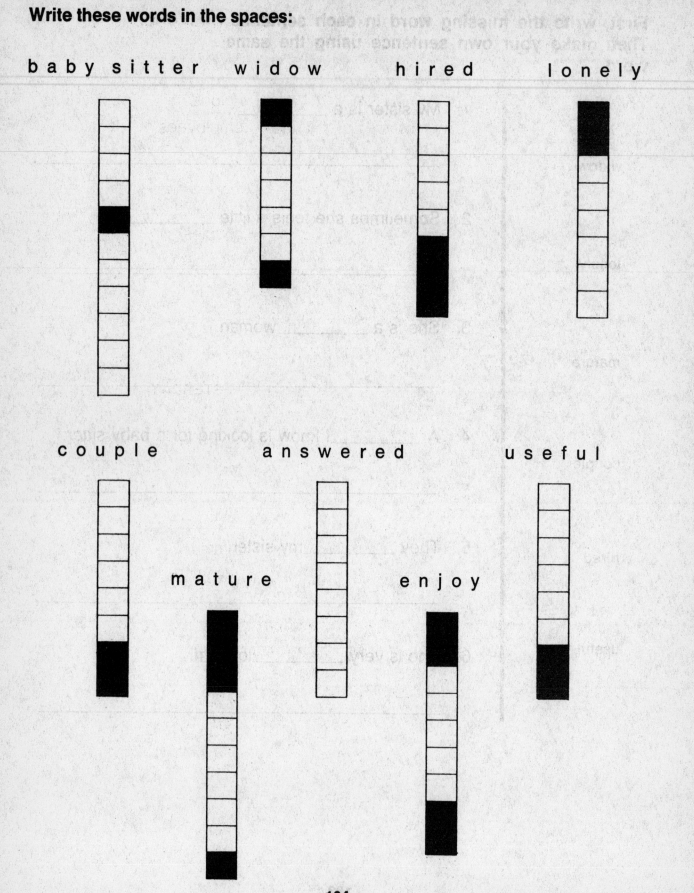

c o u p l e   a n s w e r e d   u s e f u l

m a t u r e   e n j o y

ONE

account

rule

_____

_____

service

shop steward

tax return

_____

complaint

MORE THAN ONE

_____

_____

unions

employees

_____

_____

_____

couples

_____

TODAY

belong

_____

_____

deduct

fill

_____

pay

depend

_____

answer

YESTERDAY

_____

sent

told

_____

_____

mailed

_____

_____

used

_____

Practice

Check the words you know:

___everyone

___driver's license

___application

___items

___truthfully

___issued

___rules

___traffic

___correctly

___obeyed

___account

___savings account

___interest

___services

___tell

___early

___evening

___meeting

___federal

___tax return

___file

___amount

___depends

___fill

___short

___figure

___Internal Revenue Office

___entire

___mailed

___union

___electrical

___special parts

___employees

___dues

___deducted

___shop steward

___complaints

___overtime

___increase

___baby sitter

___widow

___lonely

___answered

___mature

___couple

___hired

___useful

From the list on page 166, pick out the words that start with the same letter and write them in the spaces. The first one is filled out for you.

a

account

_____

_____

b

_____

c

_____

_____

_____

d

_____

_____

_____

e

_____

_____

_____

f

_____

_____

_____

_____

h

_____

i

_____

_____

_____

l

_____

m

_____

_____

o

_____

s

_____

_____

_____

_____

t

_____

_____

_____

_____

u

_____

_____

w

_____

Practice

Make words from these:

o n e y v e r e _____

s e l i c e n _____

d e n e d e _____

t a c o n u c _____

t h o s e c l _____

t i y c _____

r a y e _____

t r e n u r _____

e d u s _____

r a c e s i n e _____

n o n i n u _____

Practice

Fill in the missing words:

1. Everyone who drives a car must have a driver's_____.

2. Then I took a driving test with an examiner to_____that I knew how to drive a car.

3. A savings _____is a good way to keep money safe until it is needed to pay a _____.

4. The _____of tax you pay depends upon the_____of money received during the last year.

5. My friend runs a small _____and has a part-time job.

6. Our _____belong to a union.

7. Most of us go to the _____meetings once a month.

8. My sister is a _____.

9. She answered an ad for a _____ _____.

10. I work in a large _____.

Practice

Make words from each of these:

ow

_____
_____
_____

ike

_____
_____
_____

ake

_____
_____
_____

each

_____
_____
_____

ound

_____
_____
_____

ong

_____
_____
_____

ork

_____
_____
_____

ill

_____
_____
_____

art

_____
_____
_____

eel

_____
_____
_____
_____

ore

_____
_____
_____
_____

ift

_____
_____
_____
_____

This is an alphabetical list of the words in this book.
Check the words you know:

a
___about
___account
___active
___add
___address
___ads
___advertisements
___advertised
___age
___ago
___alert
___amount
___answered
___application
___arrange

b
___baby sitter
___ball players
___batting average
___baseball
___believes
___birthstone
___budget
___business
___buyer

c
___candidates
___carefully
___carrots
___chance
___changed
___checks
___choose
___chose
___clear

___clothes
___cold
___cover
___company

d
___decided
___deducted
___degrees
___dentist
___depends
___depositors
___depended
___difference
___diet
___doctor
___drain
___driver
___duty

e
___earned
___earrings
___Election Day
___electrical
___eligible
___employees
___enjoy
___enough
___entire
___evening
___everyone

f
___family
___fare
___federal
___feeling

___feels
___file
___fill
___fleet owner
___flower
___fooled
___free
___friends

g
___game
___government
___gum

h
___happy
___head
___Health Department
___heavy
___hired
___home town
___honest

i
___increase
___income tax return
___interest
___Internal Revenue Office
___items
___invite
___issued

j
___jewel

l
___landlord
___license

171

___life insurance
___list
___less
___lonely
___lose
___loss

m
___mailed
___March
___mature
___money
___month
___motor vehicle

n
___name

o
___obeyed
___offer
___office
___onions
___overtime

p
___pain
___pay
___peeled
___people
___pennants
___pepper
___plan
___place
___polling place
___postcard
___potatoes
___pounds
___promised

r
___recipe
___reduced
___relatives
___requirements
___rest
___retired
___rules
___running

s
___salt
___sample
___savings bank
___serious
___services
___shop steward
___short
___sign
___sister
___sliced
___slowly
___soap
___Social Security
___someone
___sometimes
___special
___special parts
___spend
___spending
___stew meat
___stone
___Super
___sweater

t
___tablets
___talking
___team

___teaspoon
___telephoned
___temperature
___tenants
___ticket
___time
___together
___tonight
___toothache
___total
___traffic
___truthfully

u
___under
___union
___useful
___usually

v
___vacation
___vote

w
___walk
___weather
___weeks
___widow
___winter
___written
___wrong

x
___X-ray

z
___zodiac